Lake Saimaa

Lake Saimaa

IN WORDS AND PHOTOGRAPHS, BY
ARTO HÄMÄLÄINEN

OTAVA PUBLISHING
COMPANY LIMITED HELSINKI

Original title *Saimaa*

Translated by Malcolm Hicks

Design and layout Sinikka Lindfors

Map on p. 111 by Ari Suramo

Copyright © 1998 Arto Hämäläinen

Colour separation, typesetting, printing and binding

Otava Printing Works, Keuruu 1998

ISBN 951-1-15434-6

CONTENTS

PREFACE

As a researcher and general wanderer I have had the good fortune over the years to get to know the whole of the Saimaa lake complex from Lappeenranta to Joensuu and from Imatra to Mikkeli, Savonlinna and Varkaus, at all times of the day and all seasons of the year, from the water, from the land and from the air. I have had the privilege of being on the lake at times when there has been no one else to be seen. My view of Saimaa has been from the lake, alone, looking at places where the physical presence of man has often been both spatially and temporally restricted, for the present at least, or else has blended in with the works of nature in the course of time. My view does not represent any official, comprehensive truth regarding Saimaa, but is rather a collage of impressions formed by one who has been privileged to be permitted to enjoy the very best areas at his leisure.

The main idea of this book is to scan across the Saimaa area in a downstream direction, although as I have wanted to pick out certain areas that are either precious to me or important in a general sense, like the open water areas of Great Lake Saimaa, Haukivesi and Kolovesi, I have had to depart from this general scheme a little.

I would particularly like to thank my family, who have discreetly allowed me space to work on this project, and also Kopiosto ry, which provided financial support for the photography.

Now, as the end of November approaches and the waters of Little Saimaa beneath my window have retreated under the ice, it seems that one era in my relationship with Saimaa has come to an end. What will follow from it all? Hopefully, a good collection of photographs!

Lappeenranta 30.11.1997

ARTO HÄMÄLÄINEN

7

AN AUTUMN STORM

Sarviniemi, Great Lake Saimaa • December

It's a couple of degrees below zero and the ground is covered by a thin film of grey snow. Above, the sky is a mass of heavy grey clouds and everywhere is shrouded in an eerie twilight. The wind is from the north-west, blowing off Munaluodonselkä with all its might. It's calm enough here in the shelter of the stony ridge of Sarviniemi, but the wind is howling furiously in the old pines on the top of the ridge. And through all of this I can still hear the hollow rumbling of the water against the windward shore.

When I go up onto the ridge the storm hits me straight in the face. I have to lean into the wind and turn my head to one side to avoid the flying snow and ice crystals. In front of me is the blue-black expanse of open water. Cold and stiff, it is still able to bend into breakers topped by more than a metre of foam as they crash against the bottom of the near-shore shallows. They set a vast undercurrent of pebbles in motion as they hit the shore, the stones giving out a harmonious clinking sound as they move. As the water hits the larger boulders it escapes into the air in a jet of foam, freezes instantly and rains down on the pine forest in a shower of clear, icy beads. Everything within reach of the waves is covered by a bright sheen of ice.

The water settles on my clothes to form a shell of ice, which crackles at the joints as I stumble along the slippery shore towards the sharp point of the promontory. Once the pebbly shore comes to an end and the ice-coated rocks begin, I have to give in and crawl into the shelter of the larger boulders.

Far away are the blissful May evenings when I rocked gently in a boat on the flat calm of the open water, dozed in the stern and watched the flocks of geese and swans as they plunged past or the groups of whimbrels and oystercatchers resting on the skerries.

Even so, I feel exhilarated and laugh at the raging of these natural forces. It's easy, of course, when I know that I'm quite safe on the land.

ON THE GREAT OPEN WATERS

Great Lake Saimaa

Before they disappear into the Vuoksi channel, the waters of Saimaa spread out into a broad expanse punctuated by only a few scattered islands, the area known, understandably, as Great Lake Saimaa. Here the eye can range over tens of kilometres before it rests on the thin strip that represents the opposite shore. In a few places the lake is as much as forty kilometres across, and there the water and sky meet at the horizon.

In the gently rolling landscapes of southern Saimaa the rocky or esker shores are clad in pine forest, which is bordered on the leeward shores by a narrow belt of alders or birches. The skerries are low-lying bedrock surfaces polished by the ice of the last glaciation. Only in a few places do the rocks rise up to form comical little knobbly islands topped with pines, their shores decorated with lichen-covered rocks.

The waters of Saimaa are restrained by the mighty First Salpausselkä ice margin formation, and the Second Salpausselkä formation crosses the open water of Great Lake Saimaa. The most impressive part of this latter formation is the promontory of Kyläniemi, which has been to all intents and purposes an island since the digging of the Kutvele Canal in the 18th century and is nowadays reached

A chain of esker islands runs across Great Lake Saimaa. The steep shore of Satamosaari provides a sheltered harbour for sailing boats. The sauna and jetty built by the Southern Karelian Recreational Area Foundation are at the head of the bay. Joutseno in August.

The scent of habrador tea pervades the esker slopes of Ruuhonsaari at Midsummer.

by ferry. Kyläniemi doesn't look much from the lake, but a glance at the map will suffice to show its true extent.

The Second Salpausselkä ridge dives beneath Lake Saimaa for a couple of kilometres, allowing the main stream from the north to pass over it. This strait known as Rastinvirta carries all the water that has accumulated from the eastern part of Finland, so that its total discharge is the same as that of the outlet channel of Vuoksi, and the strait retains some open water during all but the coldest of winters.

South of Kyläniemi the landscape is open and the sky broader. The views resemble those of the outer islands of the Gulf of Finland in places, although the flora and fauna of Great Lake Saimaa is much poorer and more monotonous. The vegetation is extremely limited and the avian fauna is that typical of a poorly endowed lake complex, with its goosanders and gulls.

Many of the species that favour more labyrinthine waterways appear not to thrive in open waters. No more than a few pairs of black-throated divers nest in the area, and the goosanders seem to favour the narrow waters around the islands. These 'deficiencies' are made up for by a number of typical marine species such as the great black-backed gull, which now nests here regularly, the turnstone, which is occasionally seen in the area, and the arctic tern, which has been found nesting here a couple of times. The Canadian geese introduced in Ruokolahti at one time are doing well and there is now a strong nesting population.

The plant species that have invaded the area from the sea coast include the bittersweet, which is common on some of the more southerly skerries, its seeds having reached the Saimaa area in the intestines of gulls. In fact it is less than 50 kilometres from here to the sea as the crow flies, and only 60 kilometres to Lake Ladoga.

The eskers and ice margin formations have done much to determine the local flora and fauna, as they have served ever since the Ice Age as corridors enabling species to spread across the stretches of water. Nowadays their sparsely forested south-facing slopes, with freezing cold conditions in winter and the direct effects of the hot sun in summer, provide a last habitat among the sea of forests for many species best adapted to the steppes.

The treasure of springtime in the esker areas is the spring pasqueflower, which is at its most abundant here in Southern Karelia, where it is the provincial flower. But there are also other less spectacular plants growing on these eskers that are nevertheless classified as endangered species in Finland, such as the sand pink, the heath gypsophila and the Baltic kidney vetch. The alpine catchfly, which grows on the small bedrock islands in the middle of the open lake, is another of the specialities of the region.

Other endangered species to be found in the Great Lake Saimaa area are the Baton blue and large blue butterflies, the lifecycles of

Rajaluoto, in the middle of Great Lake Saimaa, marks the three-way boundary between the local government districts of Taipalsaari, Joutseno and Ruokolahti. July.

The Kolmiköytinen rock painting
at Ruokolahti. August.

The beacon beside the straits of
Rastivirta is a familiar sight for all those
who sail on Great Lake Saimaa.
Taipalsaari, August.

The ice has broken up on Ilkonselkä.
Taipalsaari, April.

One of the unusual sights of
Saimaa is the island of Muukonsaari,
with its forests of linden trees and
hazel nut bushes. Joutseno, May.

Rastinniemi, at the tip of
Kyläniemi, is a bleak spot,
but the endangered sand pink
flourishes there. Taipalsaari,
July and December.

which are entirely dependent on the Breckland thyme which grows in abundance in some places in the vast heath forests that crown the eskers. The population of Baton blues, which had disappeared from the area at one stage, is now recovering well after its reintroduction to Ruokolahti from the province of Satakunta. The transfer was successful, and the new stock has thrived and reproduced.

Although the area has a general rugged appearance, with its eskers and exposed bedrock, there are many small clay depressions between the eskers and till mounds on the islands, and the occasional ones of these that have not been cleared for fields are dotted with the flowers of hepatica in spring. The lungwort grows in the shade of huge linden trees at the best sites, and large hazel bushes are to be seen on the island of Muukonsaari in the district of Joutseno.

Great Lake Saimaa has its own well established population of gulls. The herring gull began to nest in the area in the 1930's and there were still only 45 pairs in the 1950's, but the figure has risen since that time to just under a thousand pairs. As its name suggests, the common gull is fairly ubiquitous, but only a few rather unsuccessful communities of lesser black-backed gulls occur here. Similarly the black-headed gull doesn't really take to the great expanses of open

The sticky catchfly grows on a few bedrock islets in Great Lake Saimaa. Koirasaari, Ruokolahti, June.

The skerry of Peräsaaren-kari. Taipalsaari, August.

water, whereas the common tern is very much at home on the polished bedrock surfaces of the skerries. A few pairs of great black-backed gulls nest on the southernmost skerries each year.

The southern parts of the Saimaa region lie on the spring and autumn migration routes of many waterfowl and waders that nest in the arctic, on the tundra of northern Russia or on the coasts and islands of the Arctic Ocean. The spring migration takes place stealthily, with flocks of geese and swans crossing the waters on mild May evenings, small groups of waders resting on the skerries and the air filling with the ceaseless song of the flocks of long-tailed ducks as they settle on the water. The migration routes of the smaller birds appear to follow the line of the Second Salpausselkä, from the tip of the promontory of Sarviniemi, over the strait of Rastinvirta and on along Kyläniemi.

The pace of the autumn migration is often quite different, however. If there are suitable easterly winds in September and October, part of the seething crowd of migrating birds will rush along the southern shore of Lake Saimaa, and if they run into mist or unpropitious winds they will come down onto the open water or the islands to rest. In good years there can be tens of thousands of

Large numbers of foreign freighters ply the deep channel across Lake Saimaa, having entered the area via the Saimaa Canal. Ilkonselkä, Taipalsaari, July.

Great Lake Saimaa lies on the migration routes of many birds that nest in the tundra: swans, geese, other waterfowl and waders. The picture shows a mixed flock of bar-tailed godwits and grey plovers. Ruokolahti, June.

geese, hundreds of thousands of waterfowl, large numbers of waders, thousands of black-throated divers, red-throated divers and small quantities of rarer species for northern latitudes, ranging from gannets to kittiwakes and skuas.

The southernmost Saimaa ringed seals inhabit the waters south of Kyläniemi, but although there were about 40 of them in the Great Lake Saimaa area in the early 1970's, there are now only three individuals left. The exact reason for the decline in the population is not known, but the effluent from the wood-processing industries of the Saimaa region must have a great deal to do with it, likewise the exceptional lowering of the water level in some winters during the 1960's and 1970's, which will have destroyed the nests around the pups just at the critical rearing period. Now that great efforts are being made to purify the water and protection areas have begun to be set up, it should be possible for the seals to increase in number in these waters once more. The problem is, however, that the present individuals are no longer capable of reproduction, so that unless some can be transferred from elsewhere the Kyläniemi population is doomed to extinction.

In calm, sunny weather, the traveller passing through the strait of Rastinvirta can see distinct signs of pulp-mills in the distance: the smoke of Kaukopää rising in the north-east and the white plumes of Svetogorsk, Joutseno and Kaukas further west.

In earlier times the waste water from the factories on the shores of Lappeenranta and Joutseno used to flow along the lake bottom, against the current, for a distance of some twenty kilometres, reaching the deeps of Ilkonselkä and the south-facing shores of Kyläniemi in the main area of Great Lake Saimaa and causing a severe oxygen deficiency in winter. Water quality has improved enormously in recent years, however, even in the areas close to the pulp-mills, as a result of more efficient purification measures.

The water in the area north of Kyläniemi is of excellent quality, and there the Saimaa ringed seals have managed slightly better. There are still just under ten of them. One female in particular, christened Venla, which was moved there from further north in the Saimaa complex, has already given birth to two pups in her new habitat.

The Great Lake Saimaa area is almost uninhabited for ten months in the year, as the human presence is confined almost entirely to the period between Midsummer and the early part of August. Access is restricted in winter by the long distances and the need to keep the shipping channel open, and for the same reasons there are relatively few holiday homes in the open water areas, most of them being grouped on the eastern and western shores, in the shelter of the islands. The southern shore, with its more serious industrial effluent problems, has not attracted the builders of country cottages.

Winter encroaches, slowly but surely, on the great stretches of open water. Petraselkä, Puumala, November.

Boat traffic during the summer is mainly limited to the areas around Päihäniemi, Satamosaari, Ilkonsaari, Rastinniemi and Ruuhonsaari, all of which are owned by the Southern Karelian Recreational Area Foundation, which guarantees that their use will be supervised and environmental stress reduced to a minimum. Areas that still lie outside this system of organized excursions and regular waste disposal include Kaitosaari, Huuhanranta – the longest and finest of all Saimaa's sandy beaches – Hietasaari and many other popular venues.

In fact the whole area would be worthy of National Park status, but the absence of state-owned land makes this virtually impossible to achieve in practise. The main parts of Great Lake Saimaa nevertheless belong to the national shore zone conservation programme, and a general plan has been approved for the lake areas lying within the local government districts of Puumala, Taipalsaari and Joutseno that protects the most vulnerable parts from building in the shore zone.

The broad expanses of water may perhaps seem somewhat featureless to the casual visitor to Saimaa, as it is not easy to find clear landmarks for navigation. The open, windy lake areas are also apt to send those travelling by boat scurrying for the safety of marked channels. It is perhaps for this reason that Great Lake Saimaa has not achieved the reputation as a paradise for sailing and boating that it undoubtedly deserves. Even so, it should be said that if you don't know Great Lake Saimaa you can have no appreciation of what the Saimaa region as a whole is all about.

The kidney vetch grows on a few eskers in the Little Saimaa area. Lappeenranta, July.

TOWNS, VILLAGES AND RURAL LANDSCAPES

Little Saimaa

The lake area known as Little Saimaa occupies a triangle lying between the town of Lappeenranta and the villages of Taipalsaari and Savitaipale. It is an area of lakeside settlement, villages, broad expanses of cultivated fields, buildings, holiday cottages, an almost endless maze of islands and water that is somewhat polluted in places. The main bodies of open water, Keuruselkä, Riutanselkä and Pulkkaselkä, are stark and their landscapes still unshaped by human hands. The peaceful nature of this core area of Little Saimaa is reflected best in its bird life, which includes a few pairs of black-throated divers, some ospreys and a couple of colonies of lesser black-backed gulls. Almost everywhere else in the area the marks of human activity can be seen.

The waters of Maavesi in the north are dark with humus from the peat mining area of Suursuo, while Lavikanlahti in the north-western corner, marking the outlet channel for the whole Saimaa complex during the Baltic Ice Lake period following the deglaciation, is now suffering from eutrophication caused by nutrients washed out from the nearby fields. In the south, the waters east of the centre of Lappeenranta receive a steady loading from the Kaukas pulp and paper mill, the effects of which are in the end felt all over the Little Saimaa area as far as the point where Great Lake Saimaa begins.

Being located close to a town and the main villages of a

number of other local government districts, Little Saimaa has become a popular recreation area, and its shores are now lined with holiday cottages in places.

The proximity of human settlement is reflected in the bird fauna of the area, with its colonies of herring gulls and black-headed gulls, which thrive on the waste that they are able to find on the municipal refuse dump in Lappeenranta in particular. The red-breasted merganser, goosander and goldeneye are also common here, as good nesting places exist in the foundations of holiday cottages and in nesting boxes put out for the purpose.

The meadows occurring amongst the otherwise poor vegetation of Little Saimaa provide good habitats for many rarer plant and animal species. One island in the southern part of the area supports the chequered blue butterfly, which is classified as an endangered species nationally. Its habitat has been under surveillance for years and has been cleared periodically to prevent it from becoming overgrown, as excessive shading would destroy the orpine stand which is essential to the life-cycle of the species. This project was the first of its kind to be undertaken in Finland.

Little Saimaa has played a significant part in the history of the Saimaa region. Before the channel at Vuoksi opened up, the waters of the whole Saimaa area discharged westwards through Little Saimaa, following the present-day Valkeala watercourse and on via the Kymi River into the Baltic Sea. Although this route no longer functions and the waters of the Saimaa system nowadays flow in the opposite direction, Little Saimaa retains its connection with the sea, and the Saimaa Canal sets out from Lauritsala.

The first attempt at linking Saimaa with the Gulf of Finland was made in 1499–1510, and the Pontus Dyke, east of the modern canal, serves as a reminder of the attempt at digging a canal ordered by King Karl IX in 1607–1608.

A canal running from Lauritsala to the Bay of Vyborg near the head of the Gulf of Finland was finally built in 1854–56. It was 36 kilometres long, with a drop of 76 metres, which was negotiated by means of 28 locks built of granite and fitted with wooden lock gates. A long stretch of this original channel is still in existence and runs side by side with the new canal in the Lappeenranta area. The canal was provided with attractive houses for the lockkeepers and other staff and carefully landscaped with planted trees and bushes and elegant paving on the towpaths.

The present canal was built in 1963-68, following a more direct route and with an entirely new system of locks. It was only at Mälkiä and Mustola that the locks on the old canal were renovated. This new route requires just seven locks to reach the sea, of which three, Mälkiä, Mustola and Soskua, are on the Finnish side of the border. One unusual feature of the canal is that at one point it passes over the small River Soskuanjoki.

Various exotic plants have been introduced into the area, including the broad-leafed dock and the curled dock, presumably carried by the ships using the canal. Similarly the local fish species include the chekhon, and a plaice has once been caught close to the mouth of the canal at Lauritsala.

The presence of Russian soldiers in Lappeenranta in earlier times is reflected in the vegetation in May and June, when the white flowers of the horseradish and the yellow flowers of the warty cabbage are at their best. The fortress of Lappeenranta. Early June.

The overgrown lake Luhdan-lammensuo belongs to the national mire conservation programme. Lappeenranta, August.

M/S Väinämöinen in the lock at Mälkiä. This picture is already a piece of history, as the ship is now in use as a restaurant in the Helsinki area.

The summer cottages around Little Saimaa form a fairly old belt of settlement.

One of the largest pulp and paper mills in the country, UPM-Kymmene Corporation Kaukas, is located at Pappilansalmi in Lappeenranta. February.

The wild natural countryside of Saimaa begins immediately outside the towns and villages. The purple loosestrife, chosen as the local plant of the town of Lappeenranta, with the town in the background.

There are many small patches of cultivated land on the shore of Little Saimaa. Lavikanlahti, Savitaipale, August.

THE HUB OF SAIMAA

Savonlinna

The castle of St. Olaf (Olavinlinna) was founded by the nobleman Erik Axelsson Tott in 1475 on a rocky island surrounded by the turbulent waters of the strait of Kyrönsalmi which links the lakes Haukivesi and Pihlajavesi. The purpose of the fortress was to improve security along the politically unstable eastern boundary of Finland and to provide protection for the pioneer settlers in the Savo region. The castle fell into the hands of the Russians in 1742 and became part of their extensive defence system. It lost its significance in this respect when Finland was annexed to Russia in 1808, however, and subsequently served as a prison before being abandoned altogether. Repair work was begun in the 1870's, but it was only about twenty years ago that it was finally restored completely.

The town of Savonlinna grew up in the course of time around the castle and its garrison, and nowadays Olavinlinna serves as the principal venue for the Savonlinna Opera Festival.

An old street in Savonlinna.

Next page: The castle of
Olavinlinna and the
current around it in winter. February.

AUTUMN

October in the Linnansaari National Park

The drizzle that had been coming down all morning finally left off around midday. The low-lying clouds and mist became entangled in the crowns of the trees in the still air. I shiver in my waterproofs on the shore of Louhimaa. The aspens have already dropped their leaves, but some of the birches along the shore still retain theirs, and they stand out in patterns of yellow lace against the dark green of the pine forest. The heaps of grass cut from the yard of the farm in late summer, stretching all the way from the steps to the smoke sauna and piled up at the edge of the meadow, are still a strident green.

The camping site on the other side of the bay is quiet now, and its motor boats and canoes have given way to a flock of twelve migrating black-throated divers looking for fish in the area between the islands. There is a splash about twenty metres away from me, and a dark, solemn-looking face pokes up out of the water and stares straight at me, expressionless. There is something primitive about the black, watery, almost human features of a seal. Lazily it draws a deep, resounding breath into its round nostrils and dives beneath the water again. Its broad, lithe back is visible for a moment, and then all is silent for a while until the creature surfaces again at the head of the bay. It swims backwards and forwards in the calm water for a couple of hours, fishing, and occasionally eyeing me suspiciously, although evidently no more than curious.

At last the break in the cloud that we have been waiting for for many days makes its appearance, and the cold, blue sky peeps out from between the mass of cloud, as grey as a pair of felt boot liners. A wind gets up in the east, and the evening sun turns on the yellow and blue colours of the landscape.

A somewhat uncertain-looking flock of about a hundred barnacle geese flies over with muffled squawks, and further to the north there is a small group of grey geese. Half an hour later a slightly smaller cluster of barnacle geese flies up from the south, and then, in the gloom of evening, yet a third flock, this time of more than a hundred individuals, flies across the full moon, with white-fronted geese bringing up the rear. But they are a long way off course – far too far west!

IN THE HEART OF SAIMAA

Haukivesi and the Linnansaari National Park

Leaving Lake Joutenvesi behind, the main body of water making up the Saimaa complex passes westwards through the fast-flowing stream of Tappuvirta, into Lake Haukivesi and directly into the Linnansaari National Park. Lake Haukivesi marks the confluence between the Kallavesi lake system that flows into Saimaa via the town of Varkaus and the waters of the north-eastern part of the Vuoksi drainage basin. Finally these merge and squeeze through the narrow sound of Kyrönsalmi in Savonlinna before entering Lake Pihlajavesi.

Lake Haukivesi is about 80 kilometres long and extends southwards from Varkaus as far as Savonlinna. The majority of the main islands in this area belong to the Linnansaari National Park, which comprises 130 islands of over 1 ha in area and hundreds of smaller rocky skerries and reefs.

The island vegetation features many sharp contrasts. The shores form a barren, rocky or stony façade in places for the lush mixed forests hiding in the gorges and hollows lying behind them. These almost take on the character of fresh herb-rich forests at the best sites. The broad-leafed forests are a reminder of the days of slash-and-burn cultivation, the marks of which are still clearly to be seen on the main island of the park, Linnansaari itself. The old peasant farm of Louhimaa and the buildings around it, together with the patches of field dotted over the island, provide some variation from the natural landscapes. There were numerous dwellings like this on the islands of Lake Haukivesi in the past, but they have now practically all been abandoned.

Slash-and-burn cultivation has been revived on Linnansaari recently as a way of restoring the old cultural landscape, some of the old arable land has been cleared again for fields and some has been left to form natural meadows. The forests on the islands are relatively young, and there is no real sense of being in a wilderness area at all, even though there is no habitation on the shores. A few unusual plants are to be seen amongst the shore vegetation, most notably the Siberian blue lettuce and the hemp agrimony.

It is in the national park that the most viable population of Saimaa ringed seals is to be found, over forty of them, of which the majority actually live in the area of the park itself. Its near neighbour, the osprey, is also present in large numbers, possibly the densest population to be found anywhere in Europe, so that if one positions oneself right it may be possible to watch several occupied nests from the same point.

The main information centre for the Linnansaari National Park, in the village of Rantasalmi, also serves as the national centre for information on lake biotopes and has exhibitions telling about the natural environment of this most typical variety of Finnish landscape.

Unpurified waste water from the town of Varkaus and its industries was still being conducted directly into Lake Haukivesi in the 1950's, so that the deeper troughs in the northern part of the lake suffered from an oxygen deficiency and the fish had a bad aftertaste. Nowadays the situation is very much better, mostly as a result of the introduction of new purification techniques at the industrial sites, although Lake Haukivesi is still the most severely

The deciduous trees had been stripped of their decorative yellow leaves by an autumn storm the previous day. The Haukivesi-Joutenvesi area has probably one of highest densities of islands of any water area in the world. In the foreground, Linnansaari. Rantasalmi – Savonlinna.

The spruces are gaining ground fast in the linden grove on Linnansaari. Linnansaari National Park, Rantasalmi, October.

loaded body of water in the central part of the Saimaa region.

A canal was dug between the Lakes Joutenvesi and Haukivesi in the 1850's, beside which nestles the village of Oravi, kept alive by its shop, bar, the permanent settlement grouped around these and the summer residents with their cottages more widely dispersed in the countryside beyond. There was once a primitive iron foundry beside the canal, working with ore extracted from Lake Haukivesi.

One of the outstanding buildings of the Haukivesi area must without doubt be Rauhalinna, built in the moorish style on the top of a high hill in the 1890's. The glistening surfaces of Lakes Haukivesi and Haapavesi can be seen from its watchtower, along with a fine tract of eastern Savo landscape. Next door to this house is the farm of Inha, the Putkinotko of the author Joel Lehtonen. This was where he spent his summer, and this was where he wrote the book of the same name.

The terrain on the western shore of Lake Haukivesi in the area of Rantasalmi is flat arable land, and the area also has a number of manor houses which date back to the 16th and 17th centuries. The first military school in Finland, founded by Göran Magnus Sprengtporten in 1779, was located at Haapaniemi.

Elias Lönnrot made use of the country houses of this area while journeying on foot in Karelia and southern Savo in 1828. Having arrived at the village of Mustala, he described the crossing of Lake Haukivesi in the following terms:

As I was not particularly amused on this journey by the idea of visiting the towns of our land, I resolved to proceed to Kerimäki by crossing Lake Haukivesi, rejecting the 4 (Swedish) miles of road that would have taken me via Savonlinna. Once at the village, I looked for a boatman. The journey across the lake was 1 1/4 miles and the two daughters-in-law of the house agreed to row me over for the sum of 1 rouble and 75 kopecks. In the course of the journey, one of my rowers, who was nothing if not talkative, told me that she had frequently taken travellers with their horses and carriages over the lake in Swedish times. At that time it was essential, you understand, in order to avoid difficulties with having to show one's passport and the other problems that a traveller can encounter in a foreign land, since Savonlinna was in Russian territory, to do the 1 1/2 miles across Lake Haukivesi to reach Kerimäki and the other more distant parishes of Karelia that belonged to Sweden. She also told me of one journey that she had made to Kesälahti, without inspiring any charitable thoughts regarding the Karelians, whom she described as just as rough and uncouth as they are usually thought to be in the area where I was born. There is no time now to go into the purpose of her journey or the attendant adventures which she recounted for my amusement for almost the whole time that we were on the lake. I mention only that she began by saying "No one would believe that a woman like me would be bold enough to set out on such a long journey." From this I deduced that the womenfolk of Savo and Karelia are presumably expected to stay and look after the home as graciously as the menfolk undertake long journeys.

By way of explanation, it should be said that the distance from Rantasalmi to the village of Kesälahti is less than a 100 kilometres.

The ospreys of Lake
Haukivesi form the densest
population of their species
in Europe. Linnansaari
National Park, Rantasalmi,

The parts of the esker of Itkonharju in Kangaslampi that are still in a natural state are protected under the Nature Conservation Law.

SPRING

Kolovesi, May

A warm, light easterly breeze, the first summer's day, +20°

The evening sun tinges the pine trunks growing on the steep rocks of the western shore of Vaajasalo a deep red. A solitary crow flies raggedly towards the hill of Havukkavuori on a slight following wind and soon disappears behind the tall silhouette of the Metsoniemi promontory.

The birds are singing, mainly a song thrush, but the tree pipits, chaffinches and siskins are also making themselves heard. Unseen black grouse are whining somewhere nearby.

A Saimaa ringed seal sprawls on the ice of Metsoselkä. Looked at through the telescope, it is just a dark lump at first, viewed in the shimmering air, but it takes on a definite shape when it raises its tail, straightens itself up and turns over onto its other side. There is no pup beside it.

Turning the telescope towards the neck of a promontory that is nearer at hand, I see a grey lump waddling out from the bed of sedges. When it turns its head a black and white striped muzzle comes into view for an instant. A badger is looking for his supper on the unfrozen shore.

The ice is beginning to turn a deep blue in places, almost black, although there are patches of white snow here and there. Short stretches of shore have already thawed and there are black, star-shaped openings made by the snow falling through the ice at the intersections of water-filled cracks. Two sets of old, deepened elk tracks stand out like strings of beads crossing the bay. No one would go out onto the ice now.

Cranes go through their mating ritual on the pond of Käkölampi, and then disappear side by side into the warm evening. The contralto voice of a swan sings in the background. There is a nest with a pair of swans on it, and a few idle migratory swans feeding on a mud flat a little further off.

It is spring on Lake Kolovesi.

THE KOLOVESI NATIONAL PARK

Looked at from the air as you approach it from the west, the Kolovesi area has the appearance of a vast sea of forest. It is only when you are virtually overhead that you catch a glimpse of the narrow strips of water that run NW-SE between high rocky walls. The view from above reduces the height perspective, of course, so that the whole area looks flat, but as soon as you change your mode of transport and set out by boat, you realize that you have some of the most impressive scenery in the whole of the Saimaa region passing before your eyes. The narrow straits are very deep, so that a stretch of water just a few hundred metres across may reach a depth of almost 50 m, and in the same way the rocks rise up out of the water to form vertical cliffs in places, with their crests 50 or 60 metres above the surface. The finest sight of all is the hill of Ukonvuori.

These high, rocky shores fringed with pine trees and often ornamented with boulders close to the waterline are typical of Kolovesi, as are the clumps of spruces growing in the damp gullies between the rocks and the linden trees that thrive at the foot of many of the rock faces. The gentler slopes, meanwhile, are embellished with an irregular belt of birches.

The Kolovesi National Park was created in 1990 to protect the island environments of Saimaa, the habitats of the Saimaa ringed seals and a series of forest biotopes characteristic of Southern Finland. The park is divided into a number of zones, so that there are some areas which the public are forbidden to enter at all and some where access is permitted only on foot or by sailing boat, rowing boat or canoe.

The National Park comprises two large islands, Mäntysalo and Vaajasalo, and the numerous small bedrock islets and reefs nestling around them. Its forests are mainly ancient stands of pine, spruce and deciduous trees that have been preserved in more or less a natural state, whereas those of the surrounding areas are managed forests of varying ages, but mostly relatively young.

The bird fauna of the park includes species indicative of wild, unspoiled countryside, such as the eagle owl, greenish warbler, red-breasted flycatcher, raven and Siberian jay. The raven and eagle owl tend mainly to frequent rubbish tips and places of that sort in the more densely populated parts of southern Finland, but here they manage excellently on the diet available in the wild tracts of forest.

The clear, pristine waters of Lake Kolovesi support a population of about 15 ringed seals, while the other mammals characteristic of the National Park are the otter, beaver, badger and of course the elk, fox and blue hare. The lynx is also known to lurk in these uninhabited parts.

There is evidence of early human activity in the area in the form of rock paintings on Vierunvuori below the rapids of Pilpankoski, on the hill of Ukonvuori and in two places on that of Havukkavuori beside Lake Käkövesi. The motifs of these paintings are repeated figures of men and elk. One thing that comes to mind when considering the rock paintings of the Saimaa region is why there are no pictures at all of seals, as they must have been familiar to the people who frequented the area and would undoubtedly have been hunted. Similarly the placenames of the Saimaa region, as recorded on the Basic Map of Finland, include only just over ten references to seals, whereas there are numerous islands, promontories and skerries with names that refer to the hare, bear, eagle, black-throated diver or even the cow or pig.

The shore of Havukkavuori. There is a rock painting just to the left of the white droppings left by young ravens. Enonkoski, August.

Peace reigns in the wilderness below
the rapids of Pilpankoski in the
northern part of Lake Kolovesi.
Heinävesi, July.

A rock face on the promontory of Syväniemi. The black areas are growths of blue-green algae.

A LABYRINTH OF WATER

Joutenvesi

The National Parks of Kolovesi and Linnansaari are separated by the broad lake area of Joutenvesi with its myriads of islands. This basin receives its water partly from the Heinävesi lake system, via the rapids of Pilpankoski, and partly from Northern Karelia in the east, where the slightly humic waters of the main stream of Lake Saimaa originate, joining Lake Joutenvesi after passing westwards through Lakes Pyyvesi and Enonvesi and then continuing towards the north-west. A small amount of water also comes directly from Lake Kolovesi, through the unusually narrow but turbulent stream of Ruokovirta, which is no wider than a small brook at its narrowest points but still has to be crossed by boat.

The flow entering the lake from Enovesi keeps the route open for a long time during the winter, while Joutenvesi itself is full of fast-flowing straits that deceptively swallow up the ice. There are over twenty placenames on the Basic Map of this area that refer to a stream or current. Almost fully grown juvenile herring gulls can be seen plodding about the skerries of Lake Enonvesi in May and June, at a time when hatching is still in progress in the areas further south, where the ice persists for longer. This is a species in which nesting appears to be very much tied to the time when the ice breaks up.

Lake Joutenvesi has a truly vast number of islands, and the whole area is broken up by long promontories and islands and a series of deep, narrow sounds that have developed along the lines of bedrock fractures. The length of coast line in relation to the area of water must be one of the highest in the world. The labyrin-thine effect is indeed bewildering. It can take at least a week to explore the area in detail, even if you have a fast boat to take you around.

These are the best breeding grounds for the Saimaa ringed seal, of which there must be about twenty in the area. And it is no wonder that they thrive, as the water is clean, there is no building on the shores and the current in the straits prevents any great thickness of ice from developing, so that the seals have no trouble in keeping their breathing holes open.

The ringed seals' neighbours in this area are typical Saimaa residents: the osprey, black-throated diver and hobby, along with the beaver, which lives in lodges of a form typical of the Saimaa area and ranges over a vast territory in search of aspens to fell.

The larger islands still boast some human habitation, with the summer cottages grouped mainly around the villages of Enonkoski and Oravi on Lake Enonvesi in the south and on the mainland shores of the district of Kangaslampi, on the nearby islands and beside the Heinävesi shipping channel in the north.

The central parts of Lake Joutenvesi are practically uninhabited, however, and the open water of Joutenselkä at its core still provides a sample of the original, austere Saimaa scenery. The modest pine forests growing on lichen-clad bedrock stand serene with no signs of felling, whereas the forests on the islands to the west have virtually all been felled and replaced with young saplings or indeterminate self-seeded thickets of deciduous trees.

The channel that leads from Heinävesi in the north is renowned

The promontory of Hyypiänniemi and the nearby island of Kangassaari in Enonkoski have been occupied at different times by a dairy, a lemonade factory and a felt slipper factory, at least. The dairy was built of bricks from the adjacent Immolansaari brickworks. The Kangassaari glassworks was the first of its kind to be built in the inland parts of Finland and it produced bottles and window glass for markets in St. Petersburg from the mid-19th century to the early part of this century. May.

The waters of Northern Saimaa flow past
the hill of Hirvensalonvuori in Lake Pyyvesi
on their way to Lake Enonvesi and on to
Lake Joutenvesi. Enonkoski, July.

for its beauty. There are many narrow points on it, and the nearby settlement dates back only to the 18th century, so that the shore is lined with birch forests in many places on account of the late continuation of slash-and-burn cultivation.

Work on the converting of the channel into a canal began in the 1890's, and six locks were built around the turn of the century, all within the district of Heinävesi. Careful attention was paid from the outset to the appearance of the banks of the canal, and regular rows of birches were planted along the route and other more exotic deciduous trees in groups around the buildings in accordance with plans draw up by the official horticultural advisor for the Saimaa region.

Completion of the canal was followed by a period of busy steamship traffic, in the course of which the area became a popular tourist attraction, leading a number of celebrities, including the opera singer Aino Ackté, to have villas built nearby. Similarly the stretches of rapids located beside the route, Pilpankoski, Kermankoski and Karvionkoski, became favourite haunts for fishermen, and many notable artists would come to try their luck at angling. The experiences of some of these were recorded by the writer Juhani Aho, who himself used to spend his summers at Koukunpolvi below Pilpankoski.

The main attractions to tourists along the route nowadays are the monastery of New Valamo and the Lintula Convent.

The rapids at Karvio on the
Heinävesi watercourse are a
favourite venue for fishermen.
In winter the dippers take over.

IN THE HEADWATERS OF SAIMAA

From the outback of Karelia to the land of Savo

Saimaa begins from the point where the roaring River Pielisjoki carries the waters flowing from the north through the town of Joensuu and into Lake Pyhäselkä. The drainage basin to the north of the town is made up of two large lakes, Pielinen and Koitere, and thousands of smaller ones, little forest pools and innumerable kilometres of small rivers and streams winding through the forests and mires, forming a network that extends far into the wilderness areas beyond the Russian border.

Lake Pyhäselkä is one of the largest expanses of open water in the Saimaa region, the extent of which is further emphasized by its paucity of islands. It is about 30 km long in a north-south direction and some ten kilometres wide. Its water is brownish on account of the amounts of humus entering it from the mires to the east, and is seasoned further by effluents from the pulp and paper mill at Eno on the River Pielisjoki, the town of Joensuu and the intensive arable farming of its immediate catchment area.

There are also a number of other smaller channels leading into this northern part of the Saimaa complex in addition to the River Pielisjoki, the most interesting of which is the Höytiäinen canal. The waters of Lake Höytiäinen originally discharged westwards through the River Viinijoki, but following an attempt at lowering the lake level in 1859 to gain more cultivable land, the waters of the lake "escaped" through the Jaamankangas esker, causing the level in the lake to drop more than 9 m in a couple of days and leaving a broad mud-flat at the mouth of the new channel which is now a significant resting place for migrant birds, particularly waders.

The shores of Lake Pyhäselkä are of a gently sloping profile, enlivened by the steep-sided eskers of Tikansaari and Vuoniemi in the southern part. These are in fact two parts of the same esker, the water having forced its way through in the Tikanselkä-Jänisselkä area.

The open waters of the area around Joensuu, Pyhäselkä, Rääkkylä and Liperi are poor in nutrients but possess some of the thickest and most extensive reed beds of anywhere in Saimaa at the heads of their bays and in the narrow sounds between islands. The explanation for these must again lie in nutrient runoff from the agricultural land.

Lake Pyhäselkä features the northernmost habitats of the Saimaa ringed seal. The species was still breeding on the skerries just off the shore of the town of Joensuu in the 1930's, and as many as 30 seals were counted on the ice of Pyhäselkä at one time as late as 1966, when the whole Pyhäselkä-Jänisselkä population was estimated at about 50 seals. A sharp decline took place after that, however, with 20–40 individuals recorded in the 1970's and only 13 nowadays, of which only a handful are fertile females.

A number of rare plants typical of esker environments are to be found in this area, notably the spring pasqueflower, the yellow oxytropis and the dutch rush.

The main fish species caught in the area are the brown trout and grayling, which visit the gravel shores beside the eskers to breed. The main breeding area for the lake salmon used at one time to be the River Pielisjoki and its tributaries, but the building of the Pamilo,

Kaltimo and Kuurna power stations destroyed their spawning grounds. Annual salmon catches in the River Pielisjoki in the mid-1950's had amounted to over 3000 kg, or just under a thousand fish.

A crustacean to be found in this area that is classified nationally as an endangered species is the giant freshwater shrimp, which presumably remained in Lake Pyhäselkä as a relict species at the end of the Ice Age in the same manner as the Saimaa ringed seal.

After passing through Jänisselkä, the main flow of water is westwards through the narrow straits of Arvinsalmi into a lake area that is broken up into numerous separate small water bodies by a series of long, narrow promontories. These elongated water areas stretch as far north as the cultivated fields that lie on the edge of the village of Liperi, while in the west they open out into the broad expanse of the lakes Orivesi and Paasselkä, from where a shallow arm of water speckled with numerous islands leads off to the south-east in the direction of Kitee. Lake Paasselkä, which is separated from Lake Orivesi by the straits of Heinsalmi, is a circular, crater-like lake devoid of islands which marks the passage of the waters of Saimaa from the traditional province of Karelia to that of Savo. This crater-like area has a population of just over ten ringed seals.

A further significant lake in this area is Lake Pyhäjärvi, which extends south-eastwards into Russia, while its waters flow into the northern Saimaa system at Kitee, through the sluices of the Puhos power station, with a drop of three metres. The village of Puhos is known to have been a trading site in the early 18th century and has been a focus for industry since the end of that century. At one time there was a trade route that followed the waterways from there across Lake Pyhäjärvi and into Lake Ladoga and was of such significance that attempts were made at an early stage to improve it by building a canal, but this was unsuccessful. The idea has not been totally shelved, however, as present day plans for the building of new canals as part of the inland waterways network still include one that follows this route.

Puhos is also a place of some significance in Finland's maritime history, as the country's first steamship, the Ilmarinen, was built there in 1833.

The spring pasqueflower in bloom in the eskers areas at the southern end of Lake Pyhäselkä in May.

The water of Northern Saimaa
is slightly brown in colour on
account of the peatlands in its
catchment area. Vuoniemi, October.

An August evening on
Lake Orivesi. Rääkkylä.

The River Pielisjoki also
brings water into the lake
system from far away in Russia.

There are still areas of wilderness in the northern part of the Vuoksi basin. In the foreground, an old winter lair of a brown bear. The Patvinsuo National Park, Ilomantsi, September.

The largest expanses of arable land are to be found in Liperi. Lake Pyhäselkä, September.

CLEAR WATER AND VENDACE

Puruvesi

Lake Puruvesi is bounded by the Second Salpausselkä ice margin formation in the south-east and is crossed by a number of narrow eskers deposited by rivers flowing in cracks in the ice of the last glaciation, which are represented in the landscape by a picturesque series of parallel promontories, islands and sand banks formed by eskers running south-east.

The most impressive of the esker islands are Linnasaari on the northern edge of the open lake area of Hummonselkä, Petri in the Mustanselkä area, and Hytermä south-east of the village of Kerimäki. In the centre of Linnasaari there is a high sugar-loaf esker featuring a deep, almost circular lagoon on its western flank with water that gleams with a beautiful turquoise hue under the effect of the groundwater that feeds it. Petri is an island of a more conventional character with sandy coves and a name that harks back to a possible ancient Lapp settlement, as placenames of the form petri-, petro- or petra- refer to the wild forest reindeer, an important source of food in earlier times. Names of this kind are to be found occasionally in various parts of the Saimaa region, and pits that were once used as reindeer traps are sometimes to be found at suitable breaks in esker chains, although their edges have now caved in and their sides and bottoms gained a vegetation of mosses, lichens and even sizeable trees.

The water of Lake Puruvesi is extremely poor in nutrients and very clear, so that the bottom can still be seen at a depth of well over ten metres, which is one of the highest figures for light penetration of any lake in the south of Finland. These properties are a consequence of the small catchment area, the soils of which are almost exclusively nutrient-poor tills belonging to eskers deposited by meltwater from the ice sheet of the last glaciation.

One effect of the eskers is that the landscapes are mostly very gently sloping and have an air of openness, with the esker islands forming narrow cones that stand out against the horizon amidst the broader expanses of water. There are some polished bedrock surfaces in their middle parts, and in places the shores are covered by rounded stones, arranged so neatly that they could almost have been put there by hand. These stony shores are commonly interrupted from time to time by a beach of white or golden yellow sand or more coarse-grained gravel.

The vegetation of these islands is extremely poor, with only water lobelia and quillwort growing commonly in the clear water and small but all the more dense reed beds in the narrow bays. The broadest area of reeds is to be seen at the shore of the village of Kerimäki itself, where there is already a better supply of nutrients in the water and the vegetation has been subject to further eutrophication on account of domestic waste water entering the lake. The nesting bird species of the area include the marsh harrier, which is fairly rare as a resident in the Saimaa region, while the speciality amongst the shore vegetation is the hemp agrimony, which is also to be found in the Linnansaari National Park and in the southern parts of Great Lake Saimaa.

It had been thought at one stage that the Saimaa ringed seal had disappeared entirely from the area, but persistent rumours of a single survivor have now been confirmed.

Although Lake Puruvesi takes up a substantial part of the administrative districts of Punkaharju, Kesälahti and Kerimäki, it is only the last of these that has its main village actually located beside the lake. Its church, the largest wooden-built church in the world, and the majestic outlines of its belfry, can be picked out from far away as you approach the village over the water, and another striking feature as you come nearer to the shore is the saw-tooth pattern of the roofs of the row of boathouses and storehouses for the fishermen's nets.

The water of Lake Puruvesi is the clearest of any in the south of Finland. Punkaharju, June.

65

Naturally bred silver birches in the arboretum of the Forest Research Institute. Punkaharju, August.

View over Lake Puruvesi from the shore at the village of Kerimäki. August.

FINLAND'S NATIONAL LANDSCAPE

Punkaharju

The lakes Puruvesi and Pihlajavesi are separated by the narrowest of strips of land, the esker of Punkaharju, a ridge about seven kilometres long created by glacial streams running through a crack in the covering ice sheet, with a continuation to the south in the form of the lower and still narrower esker of Pakkasenharju.

Punkaharju varies considerably in height and width as it proceeds, with the most splendid views of all opening up from its northern end, looking down the steep slope between the reddish trunks of the impeccably straight pine trees into an absolutely still backwater of the lake. The narrowest and lowest point is around the middle of the esker, where it is scarcely any wider than the road that runs along its top.

The forests on the esker are mostly mature pine forests with a carpet of lingonberry plants and heather, but at the northern end, close to the Forest Research Station and the Lusto Forestry Centre, the undergrowth on the eastern slope becomes astonishingly lush.

In June the roadsides are bedecked with the flowers of the yellow oxytropis, an eastern plant that is rare in Finland in general but relatively abundant on the eskers around Lake Puruvesi.

One sight worth seeing at Punkaharju is the Forest Research Institute's arboretum at Laukansaari, with its huge range of tree species, particularly conifers. About 6000 Siberian larches were planted there in 1877, and these together with planted cembra pines now form a dense woodland. As if to testify to the uniqueness of this place, it has a nesting population of the diminutive Siberian race of the nutcracker.

Considerable evidence pointing to a Stone Age dwelling site has been found at the southern end of the esker, suggesting that the area has been inhabited for a long time. It has also been of major military importance in the past, as it provides a focal point from which to control traffic on both land and water. The road running along it was once the main route from Savonlinna to Vyborg and on to St. Petersburg. The artillery pits and trenches that remain as military monuments from earlier times were dug in the 18th century.

The combined effects of wars and slash-and-burn cultivation meant that the Punkaharju area was treeless up until the beginning of the 19th century, for it was the Tsar Alexander I in 1803 who ordered the state authorities to see that the forests there were spared from felling. The Punkaharju State Park was founded in 1843, and became the first forest area in the country to be managed by natural methods. Punkaharju is now a nature conservation area, a law to this effect having been passed by parliament in 1990.

But the history of Punkaharju as a tourist attraction is much older, extending back to the early 19th century. The present State Hotel was built there in 1845, the Imperial Villa in 1898 and the Finlandia Hotel at the beginning of the present century. Since most visitors came by train, Punkaharju Railway Station is veritably "imperial" in style.

The author Zacharius Topelius and the poet J. L. Runeberg are among the famous people who frequented the area in their time, and the writer and photographer I. K. Inha had the following to say

in his book on the landscapes of Finland at the beginning of this century:

"What an extraordinary natural formation, like a bridge built by giants between Great Puruvesi and Little Puruvesi, a huge pike, dried-up and turned to earth, preserved for all eternity from the first days of the Creation!" Thus says the poetic imagination, while the scientist, using his powers of deduction, exclaims "What a beautiful boulder ridge from the Ice Age!" But whatever its origins, this is an unusual landscape, known of old as a marked spot. I am by no means the first who has delighted in walking along it.

The yellow oxytropis thrives only
on the bare verges beside the roads.
Punkaharju, June.

The red trunks of the ancient pines
are the hallmark of Punkaharju.

A SUMMER'S NIGHT
ON LAKE PIHLAJAVESI

June

I push my boat out into the water beside the ferry landing stage on the island of Pietolansaari, and leave it to float at the end of a slack line. I back the car and trailer into an alder grove on the edge of the field, where they will get some shade from the next day's hot sun. It was blazing down from a cloudless sky a couple of hours ago when I left Lappeenranta and the temperature was going on for thirty degrees. The first signs of rain could be seen in the northern sky around Imatra, and north of Ruokolahti I ran into a stormy front so that the rain was coming down in sheets and the thunder rumbling all around.

Here on the shore of Lake Pihlajavesi the sky is loaded with thick cloud. It is hot, but with an unpleasant wind blowing from the north. It is about eight o'clock when I start the outboard motor and set out in the direction of a less familiar area amongst the labyrinth of islands between Kongonsaari and Kokonsaari. A picture comes to my mind of Lake Pihlajavesi as it engraved itself sharply in my memory when I came here for the first time fifteen years ago. I see high cliffs, rocky skerries side by side, jutting out of the calm water, and the blue light of the late evening. The weather as it is at the moment is not very promising as far as photography is concerned, but I know from experience that finding suitable places for use in the future is half the battle.

I motor along the channel that takes me into the maze of islands, and reaching Kokonsaari, steer for its tip and stop the boat to have a bite to eat. The rain clouds are beginning to disperse and the light drizzle lifted some time ago. The sky begins to clear from the east, but a wicked-looking bank of storm clouds is bearing down from the north.

I set off again and make my way gently for the southern end of the island of Laukansaari and from their via the little skerries towards Kongonsaari. I think about making a camp to avoid the rain and thunder, but then the clouds gradually retreat towards the north and the evening sun emerges over the top of them to bathe the whole landscape in light. I land at a nearby skerry and slip on the wet, lichen-covered rocks as I scramble onto it. A pair of arctic terns on the neighbouring island set up an evil squawking, but they soon calm down again. The wind dies down entirely, and the silence throbs in my ears. Not even the cries of wildfowl are to be heard.

But most important of all, the view that opens out in front of me is precisely what I have always wanted one day to record on film, and the evening light is just coming round to the best angle. I can take my time. I put up my tripod, frame the picture as I want it, make the necessary settings and adjustments and measure the light. An hour and a half later I have captured at one visit all the views that I had only tentatively imagined that I might one day take.

Once the sun has gone down I circle round the islands again in my boat, but as the light fades it becomes more and more difficult to read the charts and spot the deceptive rocks just beneath the surface. The colours of the landscape are extinguished and the rugged shores of the islands become hidden in the dark shadows.

I emerge from the labyrinth out onto the flat calm of the open water of Paatisenselkä. I stop the engine and look around with my binoculars. Soon the silhouette of a black-throated diver appears near the island of Kankaissaari, and a moment later the round head of a seal pops up to the surface far away to the south, only to disappear almost at once. I make my way to the eastern tip of Kankaissaari, string up the inner lining of my tent between two trees to serve as a mosquito net and crawl inside with my sleeping mat. It's so warm that I don't need a sleeping bag at all. Then the silence is broken; a huge cloud of mosquitoes gathers on the outside of the tent and strikes up an ear-splitting whine.

I wake after three hours of sleep, listen to the silence and then cautiously open the zip on the netting a fraction. The same cloud of insects is still flying around, but without making a sound! I take down my night's shelter and throw everything into the boat, and then sit on a rock by the water's edge gradually waking up as my sandwiches and tea begin to take effect. Although the first signs of the approaching dawn can be seen on the horizon in the north-east, there is no bird song to be heard, no gabbling of gulls. Not a seal to be seen anywhere on the open water.

I shove the boat into the water, drop the outboard motor down into position and, regretting the necessity to break the silence, start the motor, which obediently fires at once. The boat gathers speed until it is planing across the still water, and then I lay off the throttle a little and point the bow towards Kokonselkä and on to the next maze of islands.

The sun is up, and it immediately casts a warmth over everywhere, presaging another hot day.

HOME OF THE RINGED SEAL

Pihlajavesi

After passing by Savonlinna and through the straits of Kyrönsalmi, the main stream of the Saimaa lake system turns abruptly westwards into a sequence of long narrow sounds before entering the straits of Vekaransalmi. South of this area lies the vast mosaic of islands in Lake Pihlajavesi through which the waters from Lake Puruvesi in the east filter to merge with the main stream.

The landscape of Pihlajavesi was shaped by the ice sheet of the last glaciation, which fashioned the fractured bedrock into a regular NW-SE oriented pattern of rocky islands and skerries surmounted by high ridges and separated by deep gorges that form narrow straits. The shores are lined with gentle esker ridges in some places, but elsewhere the shear granite rocks with their grid of fine surface fractures rise up out of the lake in an awesome manner.

At its southern end the lake borders on the Second Salpausselkä ridge, and the shores are mostly of rock or till, but the views towards Punkaharju are quite different, for here the blue of the water more often than not is separated from the green of the forests by a shimmering white strip of coarse sand or gravel. There is practically no aquatic vegetation at all, as the water is poor in nutrients and perfectly clear and the shores are barren and steep. It is only in the more sheltered straits and at the heads of narrow bays or on shallow esker shores that the reeds can gain a foothold. Punkaharju very nearly divides Lake Pihlajavesi from Lake Puruvesi, the clear waters of which are able to pass through only at three points.

As in the Haukivesi area, the barren façade of Lake Pihlajavesi hides behind it a number of quite rich broad-leafed forests, and there are also places in which the soil is sufficiently fertile to support small-scale cultivation. The area has a number of large inhabited islands, some of which can nowadays be reached by road and some by ferry, while others have to rely on private boats in summer and roads across the ice in winter. Some of these islands have been shaped by human activity into very special cultural landscapes of their own, perhaps the most representative of which are to be seen on Kokonsaari, which lies within the area of the town of Savonlinna and whose scenery retains features of the hunting, fishing and gathering economy of earlier times and of traditional agriculture. Being still inhabited, however, it also carries the stigmata of our modern economy in the form of clear felling, forest ditching and contemporary buildings.

The islands in Lake Pihlajavesi have largely been spared from invasion by holiday cottages, and the few that have been built on them are sparsely distributed over the whole area.

In order to safeguard the breeding sites of the Saimaa ringed seal, the Pihlajavesi area was incorporated into the national shoreline conservation programme being implemented with EU funds, a decision accompanied by much bitter dissent and in contradiction to the already approved general plan for the area. Parts of Lake Pihlajavesi have also been proposed for inclusion in the UNESCO World Heritage Catalogue. If all goes well, a broad buffer zone will be created to protect the actual habitats of the ringed seals, as the lake constitutes the second most important breeding area for these seals after Lake Haukivesi.

Typical of the surroundings of Lake Pihlajavesi are the mighty,
rugged rock faces with their square patterns of fractures.

The southern end of Lake Pihlajavesi has innumerable long, narrow
NW-SE oriented islands and skerries with polished bedrock surfaces.
Punkaharju – Savonlinna, September.

The original inhabitant of Lake Pihlajavesi, the Saimaa ringed seal.

Lake Pihlajavesi in general is stark in appearance...

...but there are many lush depressions hiding behind the austere façade.

THE HEARTLANDS OF SOUTHERN SAVO

From Vekaransalmi to the village of Puumala

The waters that leave Lake Pihlajavesi squeeze through the narrow straits of Vekaransalmi before branching into two closely confined, fast-flowing channels, the weaker of which skirts round the island of Partalansalmi in an anticlockwise direction while the more powerful one does so in a clockwise direction, via its eastern and southern sides.

This is an area of till soils with broad, high, forested bedrock outcrops rising up from them. The shores are lined with poor, lichen-carpeted pine forests, and Partalansaari itself is a remote, forested island with sharp features and has a considerable number of permanent dwellings on it. It also has a few fairly big lakes and a number of smaller pools and brooks. All in all, it ranks as the second largest island within the Saimaa complex.

The area to the south of Partalansaari is one of the wildest corners of the whole Saimaa region, and is also an important breeding area for the ringed seal. The land is owned by the large timber companies, and the shores have so far been preserved almost entirely in a natural state.

The atmosphere in this area is indeed one of a wilderness of virgin forests, in spite of the felled areas on the mainland that scar the landscape practically wherever one goes, for many of the islands possess small clumps of naturally growing pines that evidently include many trees of a substantial age. The rocky shores, the gnarled pines, the maze of islands and skerries, the more gently sloping esker shores in the southern part of the area and the blue of the high hills rising in the distance create a landscape that is utterly unique. The most breathtaking views are to be found at Enkelinniemi, where the long rock face of Pukarinmäki rises vertically out of the water to a height of almost 60 m. Just off the shore there is a precipitous islet with the appearance of a natural fortress, known appropriately as Pieni Linnasaari, the small castle island.

One cannot come any closer than this in Southern Finland to the feeling of being out in the wild. There must be far more bears and ringed seals than people living within a radius of 5 kilometres from this spot, and the water quality is probably the nearest to the natural situation of any part of the Saimaa lake system. The backcloth to all this is formed by the high watershed area that divides the Saimaa basin from that of Lake Ladoga, rising up bleakly behind the Second Salpausselkä ridge, well into the district of Ruokolahti.

If one moves about sufficiently silently there are a whole host of wild animals, fish and birds to be seen here: a ringed seal fishing in the open water, a bear, an otter, an osprey, hobby, or a black-throated diver. The oldest pair of ospreys in the area have been nesting on the same skerry since 1971. The deep croak of the raven and the grating shout of the black woodpecker are inherent elements of the auditory landscape of this area. A small colony of herring gulls can also be heard chattering on some of the islets during the summer.

Passing on westwards, we come to the long, narrow bays of Viljakansaari, which form a labyrinth that appears to come to a dead-end. There are in fact two exits, however, a western route leading into Lake Ummistonvesi and through an open canal almost directly to the village of Puumala, and another into Soutusalmi, which opens out to the south, leading to the Kukonharju canal, built by Russian troops in the 18th century. This second route leads eventually through a narrow, winding channel to the Käyhkää canal and from there to the open waters of Great Lake Saimaa. This route formed part of the Russian system of fortresses designed to protect traffic between Lappeenranta and Savonlinna as it passed through the straits of Puumalansalmi, where the boundary defined by the Treaty of Turku in 1743 was controlled by the Swedes.

Another significant view in this area between Lake Pihlajavesi and the straits of Puumalansalmi is of the village of Sulkava, located on a minor waterway route leading from the north. The church and the street running along the shore, with its buildings, represent everything that is most beautiful in the Saimaa countryside.

On the northern shore of the Hakovirta channel, close to the village of Sulkava, are the remains of the 14th century Linnavuori castle, one of the best-known of Finland's ancient fortresses and one of the twelve existing in the Saimaa region. All that is left of the castle nowadays is a grey granite wall about a metre high that encircles the summit of the hill.

The hill of Linnavuori rises up out of the water as a vertical wall to a height of 57 metres, with magnificent views of the lake scenery opening up towards Lake Enonvesi and over the forested hills of Partalansaari on the opposite shore. This was a place of protection and defence in its time, a place where one could retreat from danger when an enemy threatened. The signs of ancient settlement here include the promontory of Keriniemi in the south-west corner of Partalansaari, where an ancient dwelling site has been discovered on the shore terrace beside the eskers. Palaeobotanists have confirmed that settlement in the Sulkava area does indeed go back a long way in time, as grain cultivation became established in the area as early as the 12th century.

The main stream that passes the island of Partalansaari runs directly westwards into the fast-flowing strait of Kietävälänsalmi, and eventually the village of Puumala comes into sight on this route, too. It is impossible, in any case, to pass the village without noticing it, as the strait is crossed at that point by the massive Saimaa Bridge, built in 1995.

The village is a busy place when the summer residents are visiting it and filling all the public moorings with their boats. This is in a way merely a continuation of an old tradition, as Puumala was an important junction in the Lake Saimaa shipping network around the turn of the century and was famous as a harbour for the loading of timber for export and as an overnight stop on the shipping route between Kuopio and St.Petersburg.

The straits at Puumala have also played an important part in Finland's military history, as for a long time they marked the boundary between the territories of Sweden and Russia. It was just south of here, in Vuolteensalmi, that a staged offensive by the Swedes against their own troops on 28.6.1788 served as a pretext for the commencement of a war with Russia that lasted for a couple of years during the reign of King Gustav III.

Morning on the island of
Katossaari. Puumala, July.

Ramparts surrounding the top
of the Linnavuori hill at Pisa-
malahti. Sulkava, September.

The shores of Lake Saimaa often provide very poor growing sites for plants. Muikunselkä, Puumala, May.

Bedrock islands in the Katosselkä area. This is one of the most impressive wilderness landscapes in Southern Finland. Puumala, August.

The harbour at Puumala is deserted in winter, but the current keeps the water free of ice all the year round. January.

The main stream of the Saimaa
lake system flows east of
the island of Partalansaari.
Sulkava, April.

THE CRADLE OF HUMAN SETTLEMENT

Louhivesi and Yövesi

There are two crescent-shaped bodies of water located on the divide between the Kymi and Vuoksi waterway systems: Lake Louhivesi in the north and Lake Yövesi in the south. Louhivesi then continues westward in the form of a channel leading to the town of Mikkeli, while Yövesi begins at the village of Ristiina and continues east, merging with Great Lake Saimaa.

The waters of the area around Mikkeli have a characteristically abundant aquatic vegetation, as the naturally fertile clay soils of the flanks of the eskers that reach down to the shores receive further nutrients from the town's domestic waste water. Indicators of a high nutrient content include above all the lush stands of reeds, bulrushes and reed sweet-grass.

The bird life of this area is composed mainly of wetland species. Huge colonies of great crested grebes nest in places among the reeds in an area stretching as far as the western parts of Lake Louhivesi, and these are often accompanied by small communities of black-headed gulls. The most eutrophic heads of bays close to Mikkeli provide nesting sites for coots, and the bulrush stands occasionally for moorhens. The reed beds are occupied by a thriving population of sedge warblers.

At the eastern end of Lake Louhivesi, where the open water begins, the influence of these nutrients dies out, the water becomes clear and the reed beds give way to the more modest shore biotopes typical of most parts of the Saimaa region. The great crested grebes, too, give way to the more robust black-throated divers.

The shores of the Lakes Louhivesi and Yövesi have been occupied by human settlements for a very long time and are now favourites with builders of summer cottages as well. The oldest agricultural land in the whole of Savo is to be found around Savilahti, south of Mikkeli, and numerous ancient burial or dwelling sites have been discovered there. The oldest known church building in Savo, the stone sacristy of Mikkeli, the origins of which go back to around 1320, stands on the side of a hill only a stone's throw from the head of the bay that thrusts its way furthest into the Savilahti area. There are also fine rock paintings, burial mounds, hill forts and dwelling sites to be seen beside the arms of Saimaa, especially in the parts of Lake Yövesi in the district of Ristiina. The largest single rock painting in the Nordic Countries is located here, on the vertical south-facing surface of a bedrock outcrop at Astuvansalmi, and here is another, almost as large, at Uittamonsalmi nearby.

A beautiful esker that crosses fertile agricultural land and waterways with a lush shore vegetation in the area south of Mikkeli marks the route of the old trunk road from that town to Lappeenranta and on to St.Petersburg. This esker of Porrassalmi was also the site of a famous battle in Finnish history, when the Swedish and Finnish troops repelled an attack by a Russian army of ten times their strength in June 1789. The Russian troops on this occasion were led by a Finn, Major-General Göran Magnus Sprengtporten, a supporter of Finnish independence who had changed sides for this reason. The wound that he sustained in this battle gave rise to the saying in Finnish that one can be "bitten by one's own dogs", as fighting against him were the very men of the Savo Brigade that he

Stones caught up in the current of the meltwater from the ice sheet have eroded this "devil's churn" in the bedrock at Pursiala. Mikkeli, September.

The alpine milk-vetch, which is otherwise scarcely found anywhere in the south of Finland, is fairly common on the eskers around Mikkeli.

The oldest areas of arable land in Savo are located at the head of the bay of Savilahti. Tuukkala, Rural District of Mikkeli, June.

The River Urpolanjoki, which flows into the Saimaa lake system, has cut a channel deep into the esker deposits.

Lake Yövesi is outstanding for its steep shores and vertical rock faces, which are favourite nesting places for ravens. Ristiina, August.

The Louhivesi – Yövesi area has numerous prehistoric burial sites marked by stone circles. Haukkivuori, Ristiina, August.

himself had trained. The Russians nevertheless achieved their breakthrough a week later. One of the commanders of the Savo troops, Captain von Döbeln, was wounded in the forehead in this encounter and was obliged thereafter to wear the black headscarf which has become the hallmark of all the pictures of him handed down to posterity. The Porrassalmi esker is under a protection order nowadays and the road running along it is preserved as a museum.

Another place of interest at the head of Lake Yövesi in the district of Ristiina is the ruins of the castle known as Brahenlinna, a memorial of the site from which Count Pehr Brahe governed the province assigned to him in the 17th century. This site is also significant for the natural history of the region, as the waters of Saimaa once drained into the River Kymijoki via the small lake Matkuslampi prior to the opening of the channel at Vuoksi.

The Yövesi area is a typical southern Savo landscape, with its small, stony fields, its buildings arranged in squares on south-facing slopes on the edges of the fields, and its forests with patches of water gleaming in between them almost everywhere. These forests are either elegant pine woods or well spaced, mature mixed forests that owe their origin to earlier slash-and-burn cultivation.

Lake Yövesi itself is located in a deep, steep-sided bedrock rupture, and its landscape is dominated by abrupt walls of grey granite with scarcely any vegetation cover. It is at Käenniemenselkä in this lake that the deepest point in the whole Saimaa complex occurs, reaching 82 m.

HILLS AND BROAD ESKERS

Luonteri and Lietvesi

The view that opens up over Lake Luonteri from the top of the hill of Neitvuori has all the basic elements of a southern Savo landscape: rocky shores, labyrinthine waterways sparkling in patches amidst the green mass of the forest, and the forests themselves of an open, poor mixed type dominated by birch and pine, the aftermath of slash-and-burn cultivation. Blue-green spruce stands colour the depressions between bedrock outcrops and the damp, shady north-facing flanks of the rocks and till mounds.

The summit of Neitvuori rises more than a hundred metres above the surface of Lake Saimaa which lies at its foot, and you can see a prodigious distance from its southern tip on a clear day: south-westwards towards Mikkeli, over more undulating forest areas, and southwards and south-eastwards over the sharply twisted hills. To the south lies Lake Luonteri, with its open waters and rocky islands, while the view to the north is obstructed by the main body of Neitvuori itself and the dense pine forest. The scene from the summit is truly astounding, perhaps more impressive than any other in the whole Saimaa region.

The village of Anttola, which huddles in the south-western armpit of Lake Luonteri, was one of the ports of call on the old Saimaa shipping routes and is now a popular holidaying area in summer. Although the shores of the mainland and the larger islands are nowadays dotted with vast numbers of cottages, there are still plenty of barren, uninhabited areas in the middle of the lake. The water is clear and of an excellent quality, reaching a maximum depth of 70 m. The relief of the area is striking, as here again tall, steep rock faces form an essential element in the landscape, especially in the southern part of the lake.

Like Lake Puruvesi, Lake Luonteri is a backwater of the Saimaa system in a sense. Its catchment area is relatively large, however, and contains an abundance of smaller lakes, and there are several minor rivers entering the main lake from the north and north-west. The most extraordinary of these is the River Huosiosjoki, which flows into the north-eastern extremity of the lake at Koikkala in the district of Juva after cutting a deep, meandering channel down into the broad sand bed of an esker delta.

From the open water area, the stream passes southwards between bedrock cliffs into another lake area and after a series of twists and turns finally emerges in the more spacious environment of Lake Lietvesi. To the west of this route, in the districts of Anttola and Puumala, lies the island of Hurissalo, the largest island in the Saimaa complex.

Lake Lietvesi is an expanse of open water more than ten kilometres long from north to south and an average of five kilometres wide, which is constricted to the east of the broad Rokansalonniemi-Rokansaari esker area to form a side branch that extends to

One of the most wonderful views in the Saimaa region opens up from the top of Neitvuori. Anttola, September.

the straits in front of Puumala. The shores of Lake Lietvesi vary from barren, polished bedrock surfaces to boulder till soils and the fine sands of eskers. The famous beach of Pistohiekka, renowned at one time for its Midsummer celebrations, is situated at the northern end of this lake. The forests are almost entirely nutrient-poor pine forests growing on sparsely covered bedrock or on eskers.

The southern part of Lake Lietvesi has a stronger current, as it is here that the waters coming from Lake Luonteri merge with the main stream of the Saimaa system entering the area through the straits of Puumalansalmi. This means that the ice on this part of the lake can be deceptively thin and the narrower straits frequently remain open in winter.

The flora and fauna in this area shows a great deal of variety. Many endangered birds such as the black-throated diver, osprey and hobby are among its regular inhabitants, and a group of about ten pairs of red-throated divers nest on the boggy shores of forest pools in the vicinity of Lake Lietvesi. One pair are even known to have nested in the manner of their black-throated counterparts, on a skerry in the middle of a small stretch of open water amongst the islands of the southern part of the lake. The red-throated divers are apt to gather on the lake on calm summer's evenings to fish in a large, if not very pleasant sounding flock. Another noisy gabbler, a distant cousin of the red-throated diver, is the red-necked grebe, which lives on the shores of the esker islands.

The gulls are also conspicuous here. One species that is becoming a rarity is the lesser black-backed gull, isolated pairs of which still struggle along on the forested islands and the sheltered straits that divide them, while the few that inhabit the island of Selkäsaari in the middle of the open water area of Lake Lietvesi can enjoy the company of a community of about 150 herring gulls and a few groups of arctic terns.

The underwater world boasts a population of just over ten Saimaa ringed seals, augmented regularly by a couple of pups born each year.

From Lake Lietvesi, the main stream of the Saimaa system filters southwards into Great Lake Saimaa, on either side of a complex pattern of islands of which only the four largest are inhabited and can be reached by road. The vast labyrinth formed by the remaining islands and skerries and the sounds and backwaters that separate them is practically unique both for its landscapes and for the variety of its plant and animal life. And the whole setting is crowned by the beauty of the ancient island settlements, epitomized in the scenery of the village of Niinisaari and the small farm of Liehtala.

The Saimaa ringed seal. Its huge claws are good for keeping its breathing holes in the ice open. Puumala, Lake Lietvesi, May.

Barren islands in the middle of
Lake Luonteri. Anttola, September.

Lake Lietvesi, Puumala, August.

The beginnings of a "devil's churn" on an island inhabited by nesting gulls. The gull's excrement has fertilized a good growth of algae in the pool.

The museum farm of Liehtala on Lintusaari in Puumala.
This tenant farm was still inhabited in the 1970's.

The seriously endangered eastern carline thistle grows here and there in the Saimaa region, in forest clearings, on pastureland, on the verges of roads and at the edges of forests.

VUOKSI

The River Vuoksi, which begins at the Vuoksenniska threshold in Imatra and ends 140 km later at Lake Ladoga, serves as the outlet channel for the whole Saimaa lake system. It was a free-flowing river up to 1924, when the first hydroelectric power station was built at the Tainionkoski rapids on its upper reaches. It is from there that the flow of water from Lake Saimaa is controlled nowadays.

There were a number of spectacular stretches of rapids on the River Vuoksi at one time, even on the Finnish side of the border, but they have all been either harnessed for hydroelectric power or buried beneath the waters accumulating behind one or other of the power station dams. The most famous of all of these was Imatrankoski, with a drop of 18 m. This was a celebrated tourist sight from the beginning of the last century onwards and attracted many a famous visitor in its time. Pehr Brahe came to see it in 1638, the Empress Catherine II in 1772, and the Tsar Alexander II and the Emperor Piedro II of Brazil in 1885. Similarly, many notable artists, including Akseli Gallen-Kallela, Albert Edelfelt and Louis Sparre, recorded views of it on canvas during the period of National Romanticism. One of the most renowned products of these visits is Edelfelt's painting of the "Old Women of Ruokolahti on the Church Hill" (the present town of Imatra was part of the district of Ruokolahti at that time), while postcards produced from photographs by I. K. Inha served to publicize the landscapes of Imatra more widely amongst the people of Finland in general.

It is not known exactly when the fame of Imatrankoski began to spread beyond the area itself, but even the Kalevala has a reference to the mighty rapids in the words of Joukahainen:

> *"Hälläpöyrä is in Häme,*
> *Karjala has Kaatrakoski,*
> *But they do not match the Vuoksi,*
> *There where Imatra is rushing."*
> (TRANSL. W.F. KIRBY)

The significance of Imatrankoski in early times is aptly described by Sven Hirn in his work "The Tale of Imatra": *Our ancestors evidently felt a certain respect for the rapids, a sense of awe mingled with fear. The speed of the water, the din that it raised and the constantly changing patterns of its spray provided much for the imagination to work on. It was easy enough for the receptive mind to link Imatra with the violent, primitive forces of nature and evil. Not much in the way of superstition was needed to induce people to shun the whole area. People would not linger long on the shores or settle to live close to the rapids, which meant that the immediate surroundings remained uninhabited and in a natural state for a long time.*

The State Hotel at Imatra, designed by Usko Nyström in 1903, was originally known as the Grand Hotel Cascade.

It was not long, however, before a hotel was built overlooking the rapids, to house the stream of visitors and fishermen. The first two wooden buildings were destroyed by fire, before Usko Nyström designed the fairytale castle in the National Romantic style, completed in 1903, that now houses the State Hotel, originally the Grand Hotel Cascade. The hotel still stands there, fully renovated a short time ago, on the very edge of the rocks overlooking the dried-up course of the rapids below the huge dam that now restrains the waters of Saimaa. On the opposite bank there is an island covered with ancient trees, on the other side of which stands the power station of Imatrankoski with its man-made upper and lower channels. The power station was built in 1930 and is still the largest hydroelectric installation in the country. The sluice gates above the rapids proper are opened from time to time in the summer so that the public can gain an impression of the fearsome power of the water in the days when it was running freely.

Another well-known stretch of rapids at one time was that of Vallinkoski, with a drop of 6 metres, but this has been lost beneath the waters of the reservoir serving the power station at Svetogorsk (formerly Enso). The fourth hydroelectric power station on the River Vuoksi, also in Russia, is at Lesogorsk, known in Finnish as Rouhiala.

Having passed through these power stations, the river calms down and winds gently across the countryside towards Lake Ladoga. The total drop in water level between Lake Saimaa and Lake Ladoga is over 70 metres, of which more than 60 metres is accomplished in the first 25 km.

The shores of the River Vuoksi in Imatra are partly urban in character nowadays, but some parts still make up a rural cultural landscape. Having passed below Vallinkoski, the traveller begins to come across the lush vegetation typical of the Ladoga region, although the anemone zone is still some way off beyond the Russian border. Even so, the clays that make up the banks of the tributaries provide a habitat for many plant species that are not encountered elsewhere in the Vuoksi basin, e.g. the solid-tubered corydalis.

The River Vuoksi remains unfrozen through even the coldest periods, and is therefore one of the best inland areas for overwintering waterfowl. Hundreds of goosanders, goldeneyes and mallards can often be found spending the winter there, along with occasional wigeons, long-tailed ducks, tufted ducks and Steller's eiders. One regular winter visitor is the little grebe. The appearance of the rare great northern diver on the upper reaches of the river in the early winter of 1997 suddenly brought ornithologists from all over Southern Finland to Imatra. The unfrozen stretches of the river on the Russian side of the border are similarly attractive to birds, and their winter bird populations are far in excess of those on the Finnish side in terms of both numbers and variety of species.

The River Vuoksi is at its most magnificent on a cold, sunny day, when the vapour rising from the water forms a thick white rime on the trees along its banks and the dignified figures of the birds can be seen moving about in the mystical sunlight that filters through the sub-zero mist.

The dam at Imatrankoski.

Fields in the area of clay soils
beside the River Hallikkaanjoki,
a tributary of the Vuoksi. Imatra,
December.

The solid-tubered corydalis
growing on the banks of the
River Hallikkaanjoki.

The River Vuoksi in Russia, just
before it enters Lake Ladoga.
Lesovo (formerly Kiviniemi), August.

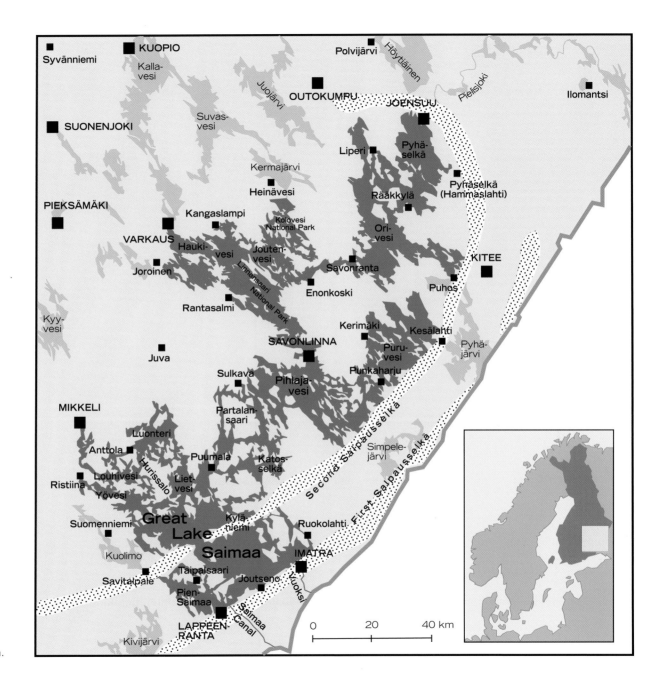

The Saimaa lake system.

Syvänniemi
KUOPIO
Kalla-
vesi
Polvijärvi
Höytiäinen
Pielisjoki
Ilomantsi
Juojärvi
OUTOKUMPU
JOENSUU
SUONENJOKI
Suvas-
vesi
Liperi
Pyhä-
selkä
Pyhäselkä
(Hammaslahti)
Kermajärvi
PIEKSÄMÄKI
Heinävesi
Kangaslampi
Kolovesi
National Park
Ori-
vesi
VARKAUS
Hauki-
vesi
Jouten-
vesi
Rääkkylä
KITEE
Joroinen
Linnansaari
Savonranta
Puhos
National Park
Enonkoski
Rantasalmi
Kyy-
vesi
Juva
SAVONLINNA
Kerimäki
Puru-
vesi
Kesälahti
Pyhä-
järvi
Sulkava
Pihlaja-
vesi
Punkaharju
MIKKELI
Partalan-
saari
Luonteri
Anttola
Puumala
Katos-
selkä
Second Salpausselkä
Simpele-
järvi
Ristiina
Louhivesi
Hurissalo
Liet-
vesi
Yövesi
First Salpausselkä
Suomenniemi
Great
Lake
Saimaa
Kylä-
niemi
Ruokolahti
Kuolimo
Saimaa
Taipalsaari
IMATRA
Savitaipale
Joutseno
Vuoksi
Pien-
Saimaa
Saimaa
Canal
LAPPEEN-
RANTA
Kivijärvi

0   20   40 km

SAIMAA – FINLAND'S LARGEST LAKE

The Vuoksi drainage basin, with Saimaa as its principal lake, forms the largest single watercourse in Finland, extending from the mouth of the Vuoksi channel to the watershed that separates it from the Lake Oulujärvi system in the north and continuing into Russia in the east. In the west it borders on the Kymijoki basin. It accounts for 2/3 of the area of the Finnish Lake Region and possesses a third of the country's total lake area. Its outflow is entirely through the River Vuoksi in its south-eastern corner and into Lake Ladoga.

The Saimaa lake system is a complex, infinitely branching labyrinth of watercourses lying at a height of 76 metres above sea level. It is about 180 km in length from north to south and about 160 km wide from east to west, extending from Imatra through Lappeenranta, Mikkeli and Varkaus as far as Joensuu. Of the major lakes forming part of the Vuoksi drainage basin, Pielinen, Höytiäinen, the Kallavesi watercourse, Koitere, Kuolimo, lying further south, and Pyhäjärvi, partly on the Russian side of the border, lie outside the sphere of Lake Saimaa proper.

Although its outflow channel has been harnessed for electric power, Saimaa is not a regulated lake in the true sense of the word. Flooding was avoided in earlier times by applying for special permission to run water through the sluices at Imatrankoski, and nowadays this is done under a separate agreement concluded between Finland and Russia, in accordance with which "water shall be released from Lake Saimaa in such a way as to ensure that the water level in the lake and the discharge in the River Vuoksi remain normal. Whenever an abnormal state of flooding or low water level is to be expected, changes shall be made in the flow of water at the first opportunity with a view to efficiently preventing any foreseeable damage."

Fluctuations in the water level in Lake Saimaa have been monitored since 1847, during which time its range of variation has been something over 3 m. The highest level was recorded in 1899 and the lowest in 1942.

A shore terrace of Lake Saimaa from the times before the Vuoksi channel opened up. Ruuhonsaari, Great Lake Saimaa, Taipalsaari, June.

Origins of Lake Saimaa

Saimaa is a product of the Ice Age, and its history is bound up with the stages in the history of the Baltic Sea. Some 11 500 years ago the whole of Scandinavia, including the area of present-day Finland, lay beneath the continental ice sheet, which reached two or three thousand metres in thickness at its maximum. To the south of the ice sheet was an expanse of treeless arctic tundra with a vegetation of mosses, lichens, grasses and dwarf shrubs. The world's ocean levels were about a hundred metres lower than at present, because of the large quantities of water bound up in the continental ice sheets, which meant that the North Sea was dry land at that time.

The climate was a severe one, with cold northerly winds even in the middle of summer. The ice sheet was nevertheless in the process of melting, and its margin was retreating gradually towards the north-west. Also, the climate was apt to change markedly from time to time, so that there were some periods that were at least as warm as at present. There was a colder climatic period of about 200 years around 10 800–10 600 ago, however, causing the ice margin to remain stationary in an area about 10–20 km wide, where it deposited large quantities of loose material transported in the meltwater to create a huge ridge, or marginal formation. This barrier, known as the First Salpausselkä formation, was one of the main factors leading to the development of the Saimaa basin.

Another static period in the progress of the ice margin some 200–300 years later caused the deposition of the Second Salpausselkä formation about 30 km north-west of the first. At this stage Saimaa was evidently a separate small ice lake trapped between the First Salpausselkä ridge and the ice margin, while the freshwater basin known as the Baltic Ice Lake, containing meltwater from the glacier, stretched out to the south of Salpausselkä to cover the whole of the southern part of the present-day Baltic Sea.

As the ice sheet melted and its margin retreated away from the Salpausselkä formations, the Baltic basin itself went through two further developmental stages, one marine in character and the other lacustrine, the Yoldia Sea and the Ancylus Lake. The ice sheet had melted from the whole of the area of Finland by the end of the marine stage, while the maximum water level in the Baltic basin was reached in the lake stage, around 8500 years ago. After that the mass of water retained in the basin forced a new outlet channel to open up through the strait of Öresund and the water level dropped about ten metres, causing lake systems such as Päijänne and Saimaa in Finland to be isolated as separate basins.

During the latter part of the Ancylus Lake stage the waters of Saimaa flowed away to the NNW, via the same channel as those of Lake Päijänne, but as the land was rising (following removal of the weight of the ice), and was doing so more rapidly around the northern end of the Gulf of Bothnia than in the south-east, Saimaa began to seek out a new drainage channel further south. When a channel did open up, about 6000 years ago, this was via Matkuslampi in the present-day district of Ristiina, to be succeeded about 500 years later by a channel operating via Kärenlampi in the area of Lemi and the town of Lappeenranta. At one stage Saimaa had three outlet channels into the present-day basin of the River Kymijoki. It is this stage, at which the Saimaa system achieved its maximum size, that the geographer and researcher into the origins of Saimaa, Aaro Hellaakoski, better known to the general public for his poetry, referred to as the Great Lake Saimaa.

The final crucial step in the development of the Saimaa lake system took place around 5000 years ago, when as a consequence of continued land uplift, its waters broke through the natural barrier formed by the First Salpausselkä formation at Vuoksenniska in Imatra, evidently in a single catastrophic event that caused the water level in the whole area to drop by about 2.5 m. It has since dropped another two metres or so as the outlet channel has become deeper.

The various water levels in the Saimaa basin are visible in the countryside in the form of ancient shores, the oldest of which have later been buried beneath the lake surface again in the southern part of the region as a result of the tipping of the lake due to land uplift. And it should be remembered that this effect continues even today.

There is no established set of placenames for the Saimaa area, at least not in the spoken language. It is common in writing and speech to find references to the equivalents of Great Lake Saimaa, Great Saimaa, Little Saimaa, Southern Saimaa and Upper Saimaa etc. We use the term Lake Saimaa, or the Saimaa lake system, to denote the whole of the basin described in this book, with its water level at 76 m, Great Lake Saimaa to denote the open lake area located in the districts of Taipalsaari, Joutseno, Ruokolahti and Puumala, Southern Saimaa to denote the area to the south of Puumalansalmi and Little Saimaa to denote the area to the west of Great Lake Saimaa. For people living beside Southern Saimaa, the term Upper Saimaa probably indicates the whole area north of Savonlinna, but it is also used to signify the part of Great Lake Saimaa north of Kyläniemi.

The word Saimaa may not in fact be used very much at all in speech, for when people set out in their boats they usually say simply that they are going out "on the lake", or else they talk about individual parts such as Luonteri or Puruvesi. On the other hand, the people of Southern Karelia always speak of going out "on Saimaa".

Climate

The permanent snow cover for each winter tends to form at the end of October or beginning of November and to disappear around the end of April or beginning of May. The snow is deepest in March, reaching 40–60 cm, and mean temperatures are lowest in January and February and highest in July.

The southern part of the lake area freezes over in the first week of December on average, and the northern part a couple of weeks earlier, and correspondingly the ice breaks up in the early days of May in the south and about a week later in the north. The ice is at its thickest, 50–60 cm, at the end of March. The open water season continues for longer in places where the current is stronger, of course, so that the straits of

The endangered lady's slipper orchid grows in a calcareous area on the watershed between Lakes Haukivesi and Puruvesi. Savonlinna, June.

Rastinvirta, where the discharge is of the same order as in Vuoksi, remain unfrozen for a distance of several kilometres in mild winters and the ice on the open water of Ilkonselkä below Rastinvirta has often broken up by the end of April.

Wildlife

Over three fourths of the area of the Saimaa region is covered by either water or forest, and the total areas of arable land and mires are small. Two thousand years ago the forests of the region consisted mainly of conifers, with deciduous trees confined mostly to the river banks and lake shores and to openings created by storms or forest fires. The change in human activity from a hunting and gathering economy to agriculture and the subsequent custom of slash-and-burn cultivation implied a major environmental upheaval, with vast areas within a radius of several tens of kilometres from a settlement likely to support a deciduous shrub vegetation as a consquence of slash-and-burn practises. In some places it is even known to have been difficult to obtain timber for building because of these effects. A third of the forests in the region had been burned over at least once by 1850.

Looked at from the water, the landscapes of Saimaa are relatively poor in terms of the trophic level of their vegetation, being dominated by lichen-covered bedrock supporting a growth of stunted pines, although there may be small patches of mixed forest on till soils and clumps of spruce in the depressions between hills and on the moist north-facing slopes. The islands formed by eskers projecting from the waters of the lakes often possess forests of tall, wiry pines, and a barren shore zone may hide patches of fresh, herb-rich forest in some places. The influence of the herb-rich forests of the Lake Ladoga region of Karelia can be seen around Kitee and Kesälahti, while the corresponding forests of the Savonlinna - Kerimäki area may be attributed to the occurrence of calcareous soils, so that even the endangered lady's slipper orchid grows there in a few places.

The densest aquatic vegetation is to be found in the shallow, muddy-bottomed inlets, where there is an abundance of water plants with floating leaves, such as the shining water-lily, yellow water-lily, pondweeds and bur-reeds. The common reed is found regularly throughout the region, although not in great quantities, and forms dense stands only on shallow, sandy-bottomed esker shores, close to domestic waste water outlets and beside cultivated fields. Even then these stands are restricted in area. The submerged vegetation, where this exists, consists mainly of quillwort and water lobelia, while the rare shoreweed is encountered in clear-water areas such as Lake Luonteri.

The scars of commercial forestry are evident all over the countryside, with clear-felled forests and sapling stands of differing ages to be found everywhere. Not even in the national parks does one see uniform forest landscapes in a natural state.

A great variety of fish species are to be found in the waters of the Saimaa complex, and some animal species have survived there which are relicts from the later stages of the Ice Age. Best-known among the endemic fauna of the region is the Saimaa ringed seal, the present population of which totals about 200. Other mammals include the bear, wolf, lynx and flying squirrel, although the latter is very seldom actually seen. On the other hand, it is highly probable that at one season or another you will meet with a fox, badger, otter, mink, beaver, muskrat, squirrel, hare or elk on the shore somewhere.

The birds of the forests and open ground on both the islands and the mainland are likewise mostly common Finnish species such as the chaffinch, willow warbler, tree pipit, redwing, black grouse, capercaillie and hazel hen. The usual species to be seen on the shores are the wagtail, wheatear and common sandpiper.

Of the species of the more remote countryside, the raven and eagle owl are definitely inhabitants of the steep bedrock faces. The most common waterfowl are the goosander, red-breasted merganser, goldeneye and black-throated diver, while the red-necked grebe nests in the water near the shore and the great crested grebe in the eutrophicated areas close to habitation.

Perhaps the most obvious and most raucous of the birds are the gulls. The common

gull, lesser black-backed gull, herring gull and black-headed gull are the most frequent, but the great black-backed gull has also been nesting in the Great Lake Saimaa area for some time. The favourite nesting places of the black-throated diver are the narrow waterways with large numbers of islands rather than the expanses of open water. The osprey is the aristocrat of the avian fauna of Saimaa.

The list of butterfly species is an impressive one. By far the most magnificent is the big poplar admiral, which is found mostly in the central part of Saimaa, while the usual list of forest butterflies is augmented by a number of endangered species such as the Baton blue, chequered blue, large blue and apollo.

The main fish species are those that are common in other parts of Finland, too, such as the pike, perch, vendace, whitefish and roach, while more valuable species for the angler are the salmon, brown trout and grayling. The salmon has become endangered in the inland waters of Finland on account of the appropriation of its best spawning grounds for hydroelectric power installations. Nowadays the whole population is dependent on stocking, as the species has not bred in the lakes of the Saimaa complex since the 1970's, and brown trout stocks are similarly maintained artificially. The speciality of the Saimaa region is the Arctic charr, which lingers on the brink of extinction in Southern Saimaa.

Saimaa is quiet in winter, and the only creatures to be seen as you ski along the shores may be a flock of tits, a great spotted woodpecker or a raven. The tracks of a fox may wind between the boulders, and the huge hoofprints of a group of elk may testify to a migration from one island to another.

Settlement and sources of livelihood

Archaeological finds indicate that the area was inhabited at least 6000 years ago, and it may well be that there were people there soon after the ice sheet melted around 9000

Paths leading to
summer cottages,
and a clear-felled area.
Savitaipale.

years ago, when the only vegetation was a sparse tundra. This must have been a rich terrain from a human point of view in spite of the rigours of the climate, as there would have been an abundance of fish and game for the taking.

One insight into the world of human thought at that time is provided by the paintings depicting animals, human beings and boats to be found on some rock faces, messages from the past going back about 5000 years. The largest single accumulation of rock paintings in the Nordic Countries is to be seen on a vertical rock face at Astuvansalmi on the shore of Lake Yövesi in the district of Ristiina. Altogether some 60 such paintings have been discovered in Finland, of which a third are in the Saimaa region.

Other archaeological finds tell of a people who lived by hunting and fishing. Few remains of dwellings or the like have been preserved, as the nomadic way of life favoured light structures, which then disappeared in the course of time.

The changeover from hunting and gathering to tilling of the land, and thereby to more permanent dwellings, took place through the introduction of slash-and-burn cultivation in the 11th-13th centuries, at a time when the people of Rome had already formed urban communities and were living in multi-storey stone buildings and going to their baths.

Slash-and-burn cultivation gained the ascendancy over hunting and fishing as a means of livelihood in the Middle Ages, but as each burned-over area yielded a harvest for from one to eight years, after which a new area had to be cleared, there were soon many places where all the land had been burned over at least once and some of the old sites had been cleared for a second time.

Cultivation in permanent fields began in the 15th century, being concentrated at first in small patches near to the houses. The oldest areas of arable land in the Saimaa region are near Mikkeli and to the south of there.

There are many sites where slash-and-burn continued into the present century, distinguishable now by their abundance of deciduous forests which the spruce has not yet had time to recolonize. The writer Anders Ramsay recounts a voyage made by steamship from Lappeenranta to Savonlinna in summer 1855, describing the feelings of the travellers and the landscape ideals of the time:

It was as beautiful and wonderful a summer day as anyone could wish for. The whole of Saimaa lay in a flat calm, without a breath of wind to break its surface. The district was covered by a thin veil of fine smoke rising from the innumerable slash-and-burn patches, tinging the whole area with shades of light blue and bluish red. We went past hundreds of little islands and skerries on which the young deciduous forest extended right down to the water's edge and which seemed to form long avenues of leafy groves at some times and bouquets scattered on a white cloth at others. It was so beautiful everywhere one turned, but the overall impression was a sad, and in the end tiring one, for in spite of its beauty the picture was always the same, and therefore monotonous. Everything was calm and silent. There were no houses to be seen, no signs of cultivation, and we scarcely met with a single boat. All that lush green splendour was deserted and dead. We felt as if we were in an uninhabited wilderness, and were much cheered when we sighted a few buildings around midday and the ship came to rest at the jetty belonging to the village of Puumala.

We continued our journey to Savonlinna through, if anything, still more beautiful scenery, and went ashore late in the evening, having spent a whole day on that rickety old boat. But it had been an amusing day, for all that, as we had fortunately been in such a boisterous, happy mood that we had not been overtaken by the melancholy that the more remote countryside might otherwise have inspired in us in spite of its beauty.

The rise of industry

The first industries to spring up in the Saimaa region were sawmills and flour mills operated by water power. Also, iron ore was extracted from the bottoms of the mires and lakes and smelted locally in the Savonlinna and Rantasalmi areas in the 16th century. The first actual ironworks was founded at Oravi, north of Savonlinna, in the mid-19th century.

The roots of heavy industry go back to the first half of the 19th century, when large-scale sawmills were set up. Chemical pulp mills were then founded in Imatra, Lappeenranta, Joutseno and Varkaus at the turn of the century. The opening of the Saimaa Canal in 1856 provided a great stimulus to industry by creating a transport route to the seas of the outside world.

The waterways occupied an important role in serving the region's transport needs up until the middle of the present century. The busy period for these shipping routes was from around 1910 to 1930, after which the road and rail networks began to be sufficiently well developed that they could compete with water transport.

Present-day pattern of settlement

All the significant towns or villages in the Saimaa region are located on the shore of a sound or on an isthmus. The region possesses six major towns, Imatra, Joensuu, Lappeenranta, Mikkeli, Savonlinna and Varkaus, the remaining area being divided into 25 rural districts. The total resident population of the Saimaa region is about 350,000, but many of the smaller rural districts double their population in the summer months when the holidaymakers come to their cottages. There are about 45 000 of these summer cottages in the region.

Human influence on water quality

The waters of Saimaa are mostly of either excellent or good quality, the effects of industry being most obvious at the mouth of the River Pielisjoki, in Lake Haukivesi below Varkaus and in the areas around Lappeenranta, Joutseno and Imatra on the southern

Water-lily.

shore of Great Lake Saimaa. Biological water purification techniques have been adopted by many industrial plants in recent years, as a consequence of which emissions have decreased to a fraction of former levels in spite of the increase in production volumes. This favourable trend is particularly in evidence in the southern part of Saimaa, where the situation was really alarming about twenty years ago. Now the quality of the water is good throughout, with the exception of the areas immediately adjacent to industrial sites.

The effects of loading with domestic waste water are also to be seen in some places, but the trend has been in the same direction as with industrial emissions. There is little loading from agriculture, on account of the small patches of arable land, and it is only very locally that excess nutrients have led to an abnormally dense vegetation. The only notable arable areas are to be found in the Rääkkylä-Liperi-Joensuu area in the north. The ditching of forests to stimulate growth is a source of nutrient loading throughout the region, however, as are nutrients entering the area by long-distance transport from elsewhere. All told, the Saimaa lake complex is very gradually becoming more eutrophic; people speak of it being tainted rather than polluted.

Nature conservation in the Saimaa region

There are two national parks in the Saimaa region, those of Kolovesi and Linnansaari, and 64 separate areas of varying size that have belonged to various national conservation programmes, 11 of these being protected under the Shoreline Conservation Programme, 12 under the Peatlands Conservation Programme, 7 under the Waterfowl Conservation Programme, 3 under the Esker Conservation Programme, 25 under the programme for fresh, herb-rich forests and 6 under that for ancient forests.

SELECTED BIBLIOGRAPHY

AARNIO, H., HÄMÄLÄINEN, A., KOTANEN, E. & RÄSÄNEN, T.: Saimaa, siintävät saaret, välkkyvät vedet. Helsinki 1990.

ALALAMMI, P. (ed.): Maisemat, asuinympäristöt, Suomen kartasto 350. Maanmittaushallitus ja Suomen maantieteellinen seura. Helsinki 1993.

BECKER, P. (ed.): Saimaannorppa. Helsinki 1984.

BERGHELL, H.: Geologisk öfversiktskarta öfver Finland, Sektionen D 2, Nyslott, Beskrifning till Jordartskartan, Geologiska komissionen. Helsinki 1904.

BERNES, C.: Pohjoismaiden ympäristö, Pohjoismaiden ministerineuvoston julkaisu, Nord 1993:13.

Etelä-Karjalan maantiedon ja luonnon kuvia, Etelä-Karjalan Maakuntaliiton kotiseutusarja, 2. osa. Lappeenranta 1983.

Etelä-Savon rakennusperintö, Etelä-Savon seutukaavaliiton julkaisu 114. Mikkeli 1984.

HINTZE, B.: Albert Edelfelt. Porvoo 1953.

HIRN, S.: Imatran tarina, Kanta-Imatra seuran julkaisu n:o 3. Imatra 1988.

HÄMÄLÄINEN, A.: Mikkelin läänin pienvesistöjen tila. Ympäristöministeriö, ympäristön- ja luonnonsuojelun osasto, sarja D 29/1987. Helsinki 1987.

HÄMÄLÄINEN, A.: Etelä-Karjalan ympäristön tila. Etelä-Karjalan liiton julkaisu 1/93. Lappeenranta 1993.

INHA, I. K. 1909: Suomen maisemia. Third edition, Helsinki 1988.

JERNSTRÖM, K.: Saimaan lokkikannat. Ornis Karelica 1995 21(1):43–50.

JUVASTE, R.: Saimaan vesialueen merkittäviä lintuluotoja; Saimaan vesistöalueen lintuluotoselvitys. Moniste 1992.

Kansallismaisema, Ympäristöministeriö, alueidenkäytön osasto. Helsinki 1993.

Kansallispuistokomitean mietintö, Komiteamietintö 1976:88. Helsinki 1976.

KAUPPI, M., KETTUNEN, I., KIVINEN, J., NIINIOJA, R. & SANDMAN, O.: Saimaan tila ja siihen vaikuttavat tekijät. Vesihallituksen tiedotus 254. Helsinki 1985.

KIVINEN, J. & SAUKKONEN, P.: Raportti Saimaan tilasta. Saimaan luonto 1996.

Koskien suojelutoimikunnan mietintö. Komiteamietintö 1982:72. Helsinki 1982.

KUUSISTO, E.: Onko Soisalo suurin? Suomen Kuvalehti 24 b/1987.

LEHTINEN, L.: Opas Etelä-Savon esihistoriaan. Savonlinnan maakuntamuseo. Savonlinna 1994.

LEHTONEN, L.: Luonnonihana Linnansaari, Saimaan luonto 1996.

LIEVONEN, T. & HÄMÄLÄINEN A.: Etelä-Karjalan rakennuskulttuuri. Etelä-Karjalan seutukaavaliiton julkaisu 4-87. Lappeenranta 1987.

Maisema-aluetyöryhmän mietintö I–II, Komiteamietintö 66/1992. Helsinki.

Maisematoimikunnan mietintö. Komiteamietintö 1980:44.Helsinki.

MARISTO, L.: Die Seetypen Finnlands auf floristischer und vegetationsphysiognomischer Grundlage. Ann. Bot. Soc. Vanamo 1941 15 (5): 1–314.

MARTTILA, O., HAAHTELA, T., AARNIO, H. & OJALAINEN, P.: Suomen päiväperhoset. Helsinki 1990.

Mikkelin lääni 150 vuotta. Itä-Suomen Instituutti A:7. Mikkeli 1981.

MONTONEN, M.: Suomen peura. Porvoo 1974.

PAASILINNA, E. (toim.): Matkoja vanhassa Suomessa. Keuruu 1990.

RAMSAY, A. 1904–07: Från barnaår till silverhår, Tredje afdelningen. Porgå. 1966.

RAMSAY, A.: Kesämatkoilla kanootissa. Helsinki 1891.

Rantojensuojeluohjelman alueet. Ympäristöministeriö, ympäristönsuojeluosasto, selvitys 97. Helsinki 1991.

RUOHONEN, P. (ed.): Putkinotkosta sydänmaalle. Mikkelin läänin lukemisto. Pieksämäki 1983.

SEUNA, P. : Suomen vesistöalueet. Vesihallituksen tiedotus 10. Helsinki 1971.

SEPPOVAARA, O.: Vuoksi, luonto ja ihminen ympäristön muovaajina. Suomalaisen kirjallisuuden seura. Jyväskylä 1984.

SIHVO, H.: Saimaa Suomen kulttuurihistoriassa. Itä-Suomen V tiedepäivät. Joensuun yliopiston Karjalan tutkimuslaitoksen julkaisuja n:o 90. Joensuu 1992.

SIIRALA, M.: Saimaan vesien käyttö. Vesihallituksen tiedotus 49. Helsinki 1973.

SIPILÄ, T.: Saimaan hyljealueiden suojelutavoitteet. Maailman Luonnon Säätiön (WWF) Suomen Rahaston Raportti no 5. Helsinki 1991.

SOLONEN, T.: Suomen linnusto. Helsinki 1985.

Atlas of Finland. Folio 121–122, Relief and landforms. National Board of Survey & Geographical Society of Finland. Helsinki 1986.

Atlas of Finland. Folio 123–126, Geology. National Board of Survey & Geographical Society of Finland. Helsinki 1990.

Atlas of Finland. Folio 131, Climate. National Board of Survey & Geographical Society of Finland. Helsinki 1987.

Atlas of Finland. Folio 132, Water. National Board of Survey & Geographical Society of Finland. Helsinki 1986.

Atlas of Finland. Folio 141–143, Biogeography, Nature Conservation. National Board of Survey & Geographical Society of Finland. Helsinki 1986.

TAHVANAINEN, P. (ed.): Ympäristön tila Mikkelin läänissä. Vesi- ja ympäristöhallitus, Ympäristötietokeskus, alueelliset tilaraportit 3. Helsinki 1994.

TASKINEN, J.: Unelma Saimaasta. Porvoo 1991.

Uhanalaisten eläinten ja kasvien seurantatoimikunnan mietintö. Komiteamietintö 1991:30. Ympäristöministeriö. Helsinki.

Uhanalaisten eläinten ja kasvien suojelutoimikunnan mietintö. Komiteamietintö I–III, 1985:43. Ympäristöministeriö. Helsinki.

WAHLSTRÖM, E., REINIKAINEN, T. & HALLANARO, E-L.: Ympäristön tila Suomessa. Forssa 1992.

VILJANEN, M.: Saimaan bibliografia vuoteen 1985. Joensuun yliopiston Karjalan tutkimuslaitoksen julkaisu n:o 77. Joensuu 1986.

VOIPIO, P.: Über einige Neuankömmlinge, zufällige Irrgäste und andere Schwankungen in der Vogelfauna der Gegend von Taipalsaari und Gross-Saimaa. Ornis Fennica 1956, XXXIII, N:o 2.